W9-AZV-462

ELFQUEST: THE GRAND QUEST

VOLUME THIRTEEN

ELFQUEST CREATED BY
WENDY &
RICHARD PINI

ELFQUEST: THE GRAND QUEST

VOLUME THIRTEEN

WRITTEN BY

WENDY & RICHARD PINI & JOHN BYRNE

ART BY

WENDY PINI & JOHN BYRNE

LETTERING BY

RICHARD PINI & CHUCK MALY

ELFQUEST: THE GRAND QUEST VOLUME THIRTEEN
Published by DC Comics.

Cover, timeline, character bios, and compilation copyright © 2006 Warp Graphics, Inc. All Rights Reserved.

Originally published in single magazine form in ELFQUEST, Vol. 2, nos. 4-18. Copyright © 1996, 1997 Warp Graphics, Inc. All Rights Reserved. All characters, their distinctive likenesses and related elements featured in this publication are trademarks of Warp Graphics, Inc. The stories, characters and incidents featured in this publication are entirely fictional. DC Comics does not read or accept unsolicited submissions of ideas, stories or artwork.

DC Comics, 1700 Broadway, New York, NY 10019
A Warner Bros. Entertainment Company
Printed in Canada. First Printing.
ISBN: 1-4012-0935-1
ISBN 13: 978-1-4012-0935-3

Cover illustration by Wendy Pini

Dan DiDio
Senior VP-Executive Editor
Richard Pini
Editor-original series
Robert Greenberger
Senior Editor-collected edition
Robbin Brosterman
Senior Art Director
Paul Levitz
President & Publisher
Georg Brewer
VP-Design & DC Direct Creative
Richard Bruning
Senior VP-Creative Director
Patrick Caldon
Executive VP-Finance & Operations
Chris Caramalis
VP-Finance
John Cunningham
VP-Marketing
Terri Cunningham
VP-Managing Editor
Stephanie Fierman
Senior VP-Sales & Marketing
Alison Gill
VP-Manufacturing
Rich Johnson
VP-Book Trade Sales
Hank Kanalz
VP-General Manager, WildStorm
Lillian Laserson
Senior VP & General Counsel
Jim Lee
Editorial Director-WildStorm
Paula Lowitt
Senior VP-Business & Legal Affairs
David McKillips
VP-Advertising & Custom Publishing
John Nee
VP-Business Development
Gregory Noveck
Senior VP-Creative Affairs
Cheryl Rubin
Senior VP-Brand Management
Jeff Trojan
VP-Business Development, DC Direct
Bob Wayne
VP-Sales

The ElfQuest Saga is an ever-unfolding story spanning countless millennia. It follows the adventures of humans, trolls and various elfin tribes. Some of the events that occur prior to the time of this volume are outlined below, using the very first published ElfQuest story as a benchmark.

OUR STORY BEGINS HERE...

7 YEARS LATER

Recognition gives Cutter and Leetah twin children, their cubs Ember and Suntop. The Wolfriders set out to find and unite other elfin tribes. They discover the fabled Blue Mountain where they meet the bizarre, winged Tyldak and the beautiful, enigmatic Winnowill, also known as the Black Snake, who jealously protects her control over the mountain's secrets.

They continue on to the frozen northlands, and along the way brutal mountain trolls attack. The Wolfriders are barely saved by the Go-Back elves. Their leader, Kahvi, allies the Go-Backs with the Wolfriders and the forest trolls to win the Palace.

The Wolfriders' lives turn peaceful again – until the Glider known as Aroree kidnaps the cub Windkin to give to Winnowill. The betrayal propels Cutter and his tribe into another conflict. Meanwhile, Rayek seeks out Winnowill, whom he naively regards as an equal. The Black Snake seduces him into serving her cause – to turn Blue Mountain into a spaceship to return all pureblooded elves and to their star home.

In the final battle between Cutter and Winnowill, Blue Mountain itself is destroyed, along with most of the Glider elves, and Winnowill is banished forever to a deserted island in the middle of the ocean. The elves are left to pick up the tattered threads of their lives.

Rayek returns to the Palace, where he watches the spirits of the dead Gliders restore it to its original glory. At the same time, Suntop receives a psychic cry of distress from unknown elves. Rayek convinces Cutter and the Wolfriders to let him fly the Palace to the source of the mysterious cry, using Suntop as his compass. Realizing he can solve two of his problems with one stroke, Rayek transports the Crystal Palace – along with Leetah and her two cubs – 10,000 years into the future, leaving behind the mortal Cutter who can't live long enough to stop him.

3,000 - 2,000 YEARS BEFORE

***Goodtree,* eighth chief of the Wolfriders, founds a new Holt deep in the woods and creates the Father Tree where the Wolfriders can all live. Her son, *Mantricker,* reopens the struggle with nomadic humans. Mantricker's son, *Bearclaw,* discovers Greymung's trolls living in the tunnels beneath the Holt. Bearclaw becomes the Wolfriders' tenth chief.**

In the distant Forbidden Grove near Blue Mountain, *Petalwing* and the preservers tirelessly protect their mysterious wrapstuff bundles.

9,000 YEARS BEFORE

Wolfrider chief Timmorn feels the conflict between his elf and wolf sides, and leaves the tribe to find his own destiny. *Rahnee the She-Wolf* takes over as leader, followed by her son *Prey-Pacer.*

10,000 YEARS BEFORE

Over time, the High Ones become too many for their faraway planet to support. *Timmain*'s group discovers the World of Two Moons, but as their crystalline ship approaches, the High Ones crash-land, far in the new world's past. Primitive humans greet them with brutality. The elfin High Ones and their troll attendants scatter into the surrounding forest. To survive, Timmain magically takes a wolf's form and searches for the other elves. *Timmorn,* first chief of the Wolfriders, is born.

0
1,000
2,000
3,000
4,000
5,000
6,000
7,000
8,000
9,000
10,000

TIMELINE

0 · 475 · 600 · 1,000 · 2,000 · 3,000 · 4,000 · 5,000 · 6,000 · 7,000 · 8,000 · 9,000 · 10,000

10,000 YEARS LATER

Cutter and the Wolfriders, having slept in suspended animation for millennia, are reunited with their loved ones and friends. Much has changed on the World of Two Moons, for men and for elves. And the elves experienced strange dreams while asleep. Cutter tries to make sense of it all for himself and for his tribemates...

FIRE & FLIGHT

The peace is an illusion, and humans burn the Wolfriders out of their forest home. Cutter and his band are driven into a vast desert where they discover new elves, the Sun Folk. Cutter Recognizes the Sun Folk's healer Leetah, and the two groups unite.

6 YEARS BEFORE

The feud between elves and humans ends – seemingly – with the death of Bearclaw. Cutter assumes leadership of the tribe.

25 YEARS BEFORE

Joyleaf gives birth to a son, *Cutter*, who forms a fast friendship with *Skywise*. The two become brothers "in all but blood."

475 YEARS BEFORE

Bearclaw begins a long feud with a tribe of humans who live near the Holt. Although both sides suffer over the years, neither gives in.

600 YEARS BEFORE

In the oasis known as Sun Village deep in the desert to the south of the Holt, *Rayek* is born. *Leetah* is born twelve years later.

4,000 YEARS BEFORE

Freefoot leads the Wolfriders during a prosperous, quiet time. Freefoot's son, Oakroot, subsequently becomes chief and later takes the name *Tanner.*

7,000 YEARS BEFORE

Swift-Spear, fourth chief, goes to war for the first time against humans of a nearby village. The humans leave, and he takes the name *Two-Spear.* When his sister *Huntress Skyfire* challenges his chieftainship, the tribe splits. Two-Spear leaves, and Skyfire becomes chief.

10,000 - 8,000 YEARS BEFORE

Descendants of the High Ones wander the world. *Savah* and her family settle the Sun Village in the desert. *Lord Voll* and the Gliders move into Blue Mountain and shut themselves away from the world.

Guttlekraw becomes king of the trolls. Over time, the trolls tunnel under the future Holt of the Wolfriders.

Greymung rebels against Guttlekraw, who flees north. *Winnowill* gives birth to Two-Edge.

The ElfQuest saga spans thousands of years and to date has introduced readers to hundreds of characters. At the time of the stories in this volume, these are the major ones you will meet and get to know.

THE WOLFRIDERS

CUTTER

While his name denotes his skill with a sword, Cutter is not a cold and merciless death-dealer. Strong in his beliefs, he will nevertheless bend even the most fundamental of them if the well-being of his tribe is at stake. His best friend, Skywise, believes that what sets Cutter apart from all past Wolfrider chieftains is his imagination, combined with the ability to not only accept change, but take advantage of it.

LEETAH

Her name means "healing light" and – as the Sun Folk's healer – she is her village's most precious resource. For more than 600 years she has lived a sheltered life, surrounded by love and admiration, knowing little of the world beyond her desert oasis. Though seemingly delicate, beneath her beauty there lies a wellspring of strength. She dislikes the death she has caused but understands that it is The Way.

SKYWISE

Orphaned at birth, Skywise is the resident stargazer of the Wolfriders, and only his interest in elf maidens rivals his passion for understanding the mysteries of the universe. Skywise is Cutter's counselor, confidant, and closest friend. While he is capable of deep seriousness, few things can diminish Skywise's jovial and rakish manner.

NIGHTFALL

Nightfall is the beautiful counterpoint to her lifemate, Redlance, and one of the most skilled hunters in the tribe. She is cool and calculated, neither vengeful nor violent unless it becomes absolutely necessary. The relationship between Nightfall and Redlance is very much one of yin and yang. Nightfall grew up with Cutter, and is strongly loyal to the young chief.

REDLANCE

Redlance is the sweet-natured plantshaper of the Wolfriders. Indeed, he will only use his talents defensively, to protect the tribe. Redlance is too much a pacifist at heart to do willful harm, and this gentleness makes him a natural to care for the cubs of the tribe. He is a master of the soft counsel, gently prodding the other, more headstrong elves in the right direction.

STRONGBOW

Strongbow is the reserved, silent master archer of the Wolfriders. Ever the devil's advocate, he is often proved right but finds no value in saying "I told you so." Strongbow is extremely serious, rarely smiles, and prefers telepathic "sending" to audible speech. He is completely devoted to his lifemate, Moonshade, and intensely proud of their son Dart. Having taken an elf's life in the battle of Blue Mountain, however, he finds that his soul has been shaken.

MOONSHADE

Moonshade is the Wolfriders' tanner. Though the process of tanning can be lengthy and tedious, she enjoys the quiet hours spent bringing the beauty out of a supple hide. Moonshade, like her lifemate Strongbow, is very much a traditionalist, strong-minded and with unshakable beliefs. Completely devoted to her mate, Moonshade will defend his opinions even when she feels he's wrong.

PIKE

Pike is the Wolfriders' resident storyteller, taking his name from his preferred weapon. The most happy-go-lucky of the Wolfriders, Pike has no grand ideals or desire for quests – he is a follower, and rarely questions his chief's orders. Fully immersed in "the now of wolf thought," he clings through thick and thin to his two greatest loves: dreamberries and taking the easy path.

CLEARBROOK

Calm, dignified and thoughtful, choosing her words carefully, Clearbrook is the eldest female Wolfrider. However, when she lost her lifemate, One-Eye, in the quest for the Palace, Clearbrook turned into a fierce and vengeful angel of death. Both mother figure and warrior, Clearbrook is an advocate of forgiveness and letting go of the past – but her path to that understanding has been harrowing.

AROREE

Aroree was one of the Gliders' Chosen Eight. When she met Skywise, he opened her eyes to a wider world. Aroree saw in him a spark, one that was missing from her own life. She desperately wanted to flee Blue Mountain, and lead a life far from its shadow, but her abduction of Windkin in Winnowill's service has brought her great shame. Through the centuries, she has sought redemption.

FRIENDS

PETALWING

Petalwing is a Preserver — a carefree, fairylike creature that arrived on the World of Two Moons with the original High Ones. Petalwing lives under the grand illusion that "highthings" (elves) cannot live without it, and must be watched over and protected. Petalwing is the closest thing that the Preservers have to a leader. Cutter considers Petalwing to be a major annoyance; the sprite remains unperturbed by this opinion.

THE TROLLS

PICKNOSE

His name was inspired by his most prominent facial feature, which resembles the curved business end of a pick. The success of Picknose's interactions with the Wolfriders has been mixed at best, for while he does possess a sort of honor, he is also an opportunist of the first water. Currently King of the mountain trolls, Picknose is ever seeking opportunity.

IN THE PREVIOUS VOLUME

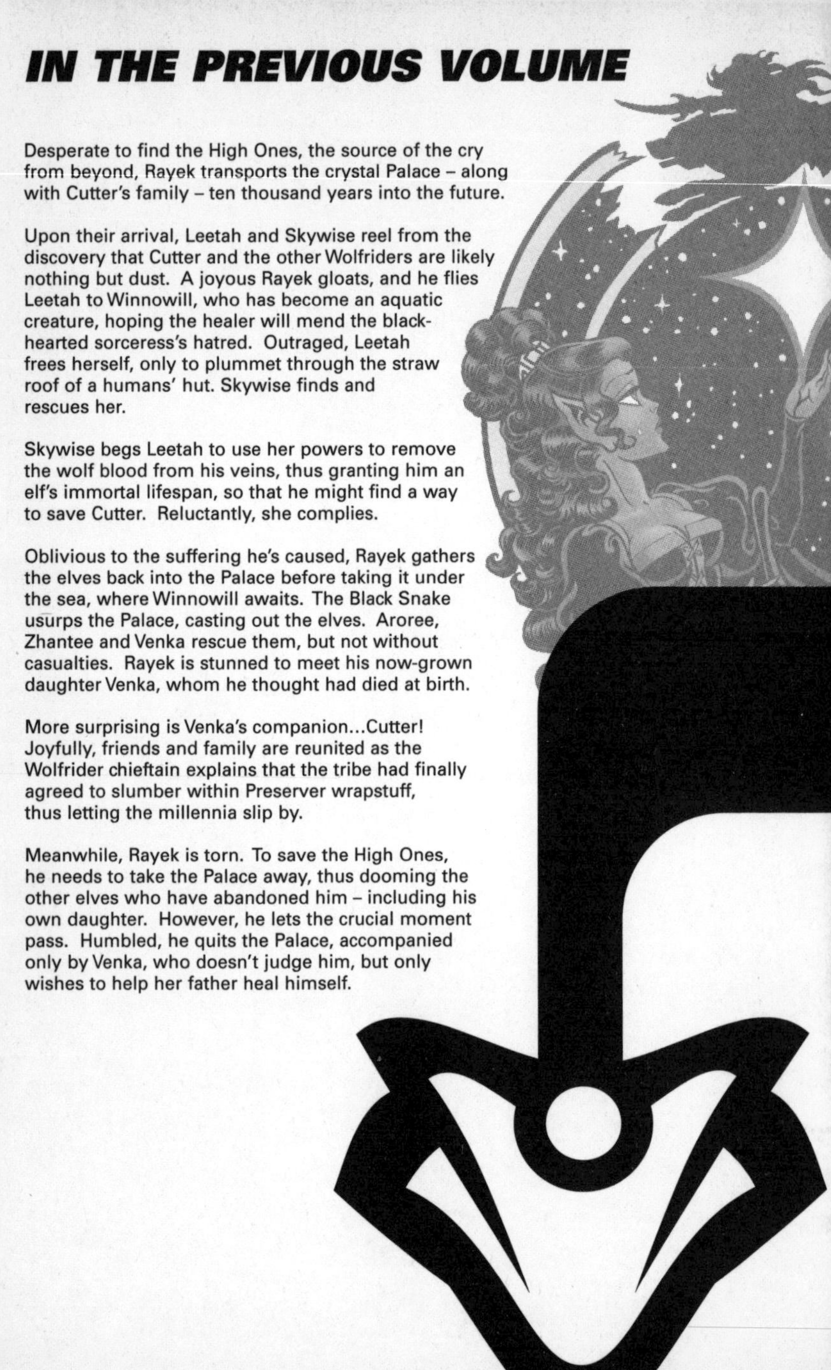

Desperate to find the High Ones, the source of the cry from beyond, Rayek transports the crystal Palace – along with Cutter's family – ten thousand years into the future.

Upon their arrival, Leetah and Skywise reel from the discovery that Cutter and the other Wolfriders are likely nothing but dust. A joyous Rayek gloats, and he flies Leetah to Winnowill, who has become an aquatic creature, hoping the healer will mend the black-hearted sorceress's hatred. Outraged, Leetah frees herself, only to plummet through the straw roof of a humans' hut. Skywise finds and rescues her.

Skywise begs Leetah to use her powers to remove the wolf blood from his veins, thus granting him an elf's immortal lifespan, so that he might find a way to save Cutter. Reluctantly, she complies.

Oblivious to the suffering he's caused, Rayek gathers the elves back into the Palace before taking it under the sea, where Winnowill awaits. The Black Snake usurps the Palace, casting out the elves. Aroree, Zhantee and Venka rescue them, but not without casualties. Rayek is stunned to meet his now-grown daughter Venka, whom he thought had died at birth.

More surprising is Venka's companion...Cutter! Joyfully, friends and family are reunited as the Wolfrider chieftain explains that the tribe had finally agreed to slumber within Preserver wrapstuff, thus letting the millennia slip by.

Meanwhile, Rayek is torn. To save the High Ones, he needs to take the Palace away, thus dooming the other elves who have abandoned him – including his own daughter. However, he lets the crucial moment pass. Humbled, he quits the Palace, accompanied only by Venka, who doesn't judge him, but only wishes to help her father heal himself.

IT IS ONLY AN EIGHT OF DAYS SINCE CUTTER AND HIS TRIBE AWOKE FROM THEIR TEN THOUSAND YEAR HIBERNATION. IN THIS STRANGE LAND, THEY CAREFULLY, HOPEFULLY BREATHE LIFE INTO THE HEART OF A NEW HOLT ON THORNY MOUNTAIN.
THAT'S BETTER, MOONSHADE. NOW LEETAH CAN GET AROUND IN THE WOODS.
THOUGH YOU HATE THE DRESS, BELOVED, THE COLOR SUITS ME, DON'T YOU THINK?
ALL THE REST OF THIS CLOTH WILL KEEP YOU IN MENDS 'TIL CUTTER'S FACE FUR IS DOWN TO HIS KNEES, HEALER!
DREAMTIME
I STILL CAN'T BELIEVE THE HUMANS MADE THIS. IT'S SO SOFT AND FINE... LIKE A DREAM.

"LIKE A DREAM..."

YOU SHOULD BE SCARFING DREAMBERRIES, TREE-SHAPER! BUT SOMETHING'S BEEN EATING **YOU** SINCE WE WOKE UP! *ULP ULP* WHAT GIVES?

I'M TRYING TO **REMEMBER**. I KNOW WE SLEPT...

...AND I HAVE THE FEELING WE **DREAMED**. BUT I CAN'T RECALL ANYTHING. I GUESS IT'S NOT IMPORTANT.

URRRP NOW **THAT'S** WHERE YOU'RE WRONG! I HAPPEN TO THINK **DREAMS** ARE **VERY** IMPORTANT!

THEY CAN **TEACH** YOU VALUABLE STUFF.

JUST 'CAUSE YOU **CAN'T** REMEMBER DOESN'T MEAN YOU **SHOULDN'T**, REDLANCE. ALL YOUR HEAD NEEDS IS A JOG **SIDEWAYS**!

NOW, IN MY DEN, I HAPPEN TO HAVE A FULL SKIN OF OLD MAGGOTY'S CHOICEST **DREAMBERRY BREW**. YOU JUST COME WITH ME, AND...

LATER...

WHEW! **POTENT**! YOU KNOW *HIC* I DON'T NORMALLY LIKE TO ADDLE MY SENSES THIS MUCH.

SURE, SURE. BUT YOU CAN'T REMEMBER **DEEP-BURIED** DREAMS WHEN THE WORLD'S TOO MUCH WITH YOU.

"JUST RELAX, LIKE ME. LET YOUR MIND WANDER..."

"...TO THE BANKS OF THE DREAM RIVER. STOP THERE. ASK FOR WHAT'S PAST TO FLOAT BY AGAIN."
MMMM... PERCHED ON THE EDGE... BETWEEN WAKING AND SLEEPING...
"I SEE... AAAH! NOW I REMEMBER...!"
"I AM THE SPIRIT OF THE FATHER TREE... IN THE HOLT WHERE WE WERE BORN! MY BODY IS OLD BEYOND TELLING. BARK AND BRANCH, LEAF AND DEEP-BURIED ROOT DRAW THEIR LIFE FROM THE SOIL, AND FROM EVERY LIVING THING AROUND THEM!"
"I GIVE BREATH TO ALL CREATURES DWELLING NEAR ME AND IN ME. I AM CONNECTED TO MANY OTHERS SUCH AS I! IN THE FOREST, WHAT ONE FEELS, ALL FEEL."
"THE KNOWING IS DEEP AND UNQUESTIONING -- LIKE A LOCK-SEND THAT NEVER ENDS. THERE IS NO LONELINESS, NO SUCH THING AS SEPARATION."

"LOOK! AS THEY HAVE DONE FOR GENERATIONS, WOLFRIDERS RACE AWAY FROM THE HOLT ON THEIR NIGHTLY HUNT! I WISH THEM WELL AS THEY GO TO KEEP THE FOREST'S LIVING THINGS IN BALANCE."
"SPIRITS FILL ME FROM ROOTS TO TOP LEAVES! ALL THOSE WHO HAVE DWELT WITHIN ME -- THEY ARE WITH ME STILL!"
"EVEN BEYOND DEATH GOODTREE, MY SHAPER, LENDS HER POWERS SO MY BODY CONTINUES TO GROW IN FORMS THAT MEAN "HOME" TO THE ELVES."

"AS THE YEARS PASS IN THEIR MANY EIGHTS-OF-EIGHT, SEASONS CHANGING IN ENDLESS CYCLES, LIVING TREE-SHAPERS WORK WITH THE SPIRITS TO KEEP ME AND MY BRETHREN HEALTHY AND STRONG."
"THIS IS WHAT IT IS TO BE TRULY IMMORTAL, FOR EVEN THE WHITE COLD MEANS NOT DEATH, ONLY SLEEP..."
"...AND NOT SOLELY FOR ME AND MY FELLOW TREES, BUT FOR THOSE WHO REST INSIDE ME, SAFE AND WARM, AWAITING THE TIME OF NEW GREEN."
"LOVE FOR THESE 'SEEDLINGS' OF MINE COURSES THROUGH MY LIMBS EVEN AS THE SAP THEY CALL BLOOD PULSES THROUGH THEIR VEINS."
"BUT THEN... ONE DAY... SPARKS! SPARKS OF FIRE BORNE ON THE WIND! THEY TOUCH MY LEAVES, CLING TO MY BARK -- AND BURN!"
"MY BROTHERS AT THE FOREST'S EDGE CRY OUT: HUMANS! THE ONE CALLED SPIRIT MAN AND HIS FOLLOWERS! THEY HAVE DONE THIS!"
"POOR SOULS! DON'T THEY KNOW? THEIR DEED OF FEAR AND VENGEANCE AGAINST THE ELVES WILL CONSUME THEM AS WELL!"

"THE WOLFRIDERS FLEE. AND WELL THEY SHOULD, FOR THERE IS NOTHING THEY CAN DO."
"I FEEL THE DEADLY HEAT, AS DO MY FELLOW TREES! SEARING AGONY! WE SCREAM WITH ONE VOICE."
"YET, THERE IS NO FEAR... EVEN NOW. FOR JUST AS WOLVES THIN THE DEER HERDS, MAKING THEM STRONGER, SO THE FLAMES THIN THE FOREST."
"THIS BLAZE MIGHT HAVE BEEN CAUSED BY AN UNEXPECTED BOLT OF SKYFIRE. THERE IS NO RESENTMENT IN ME. IT IS MY TIME."
"IT GOES ON LONG... **LONG**... THE BURNING! AT LAST, THE FLAMES BEGIN TO DIE..."
"...FEEL MYSELF... CRUMBLING TO AN ASHEN STUMP..."
"...LIFE FORCE... ALL BUT DRAINED... FROM ME AND MY BRETHREN...!"
"...SPIRITS OF ALL TREE-SHAPERS... HELP US...!"

"DOWN BENEATH THE SCORCHED FOREST FLOOR, DOWN WHERE THE SOIL IS STILL MOIST AND RICH, I AM CALLED TO A *HEALING*."

"OH, SEE! OUR *ROOTS*! OUR ROOTS HAVEN'T BEEN DESTROYED! I KNOW NOW, MY BRETHREN AND I WILL GROW BACK! IT WILL TAKE MANY, MANY EIGHTS OF SEASONS, A LONG, SLOW, UPWARD CLIMB TO THE LIGHT."

BUT, SOMEDAY, ALL SHALL BE AS IT WAS. THE WOLFRIDERS, THE CHILDREN BORN IN MY WOODEN WOMB, WILL RETURN TO ME.

≋SNIFFLE≋ BEAUTIFUL! WHAT A BEAUTIFUL DREAM!

I HOPE WE *CAN* GO HOME TO OUR BIRTH-HOLT AND SEE THE FATHER TREE REGROWN!

TREES ARE LIKE HIGH ONES, I GUESS. ≋SNIFF≋ THEY LIVE FOREVER!

SOMETHING... SOMETHING *ELSE* IS COMING...!

"THE HOLT IS DESERTED. THE WOLFRIDERS WERE HERE, BUT THEY HAVE GONE AGAIN."
"A NEW THREAT APPROACHES..."
"HUMANS! HUMANS COME AT ME AND MY BRETHREN WITH WEAPONS OF METAL! THE ONE THING THAT CAN DESTROY US UTTERLY!"
"TERRIBLE, LONG, SHARP-TOOTHED BLADES...!"
"NOW THERE IS PAIN, RESENTMENT AND FEAR, FOR THE METAL BLADES ARE MAN-MADE AND WITH DARK INTENT..."
"...AND THE HUMANS WILL NOT STOP 'TIL THE DESTRUCTION IS COMPLETE!"

"OOOHHH... I'M BLEEDING...! CUT IN TWO!"
"HAVE PITY, YOU MEN OF DAYS TO COME!"
"NOW I TRULY DIE, MY HEART-ROOT RIPPED OUT BY A SMOKE-BELCHING, METAL BEAST LIKE NONE THE FOREST HAS EVER SEEN!"
"WOLFRIDERS! LOVING SPIRITS! FARE WELL! I DIE FOREVER!"
AAAAAH!!
REDLANCE! IT'S ME! YOU'RE SAFE! COME ON, WAKE UP!
HUH?! WHA--?!

REDLANCE! WHAT'S WRONG?
NOTHING, CUTTER! JUST A BAD DREAM!
BELOVED, ARE YOU ALL RIGHT?
I'VE NEVER HEARD YOU CRY OUT SO!
I'VE NEVER SEEN -- OR FELT -- THE THINGS I DID THIS EVENING.
QUICKLY, REDLANCE AND PIKE EXPLAIN...
GETTING TORN OUT BY THE ROOTS... THAT'S WHAT I'LL NEVER FORGET. IS IT A SYMBOL, PIKE, OR A WARNING?
MAYBE BOTH! THE DREAM'S UNFINISHED. THERE'S A TEACHING IN IT THAT NEEDS UNCOVERING.
YOU SAID, WITH TREES, WHAT ONE FEELS, ALL FEEL. MAYBE, WITH US, WHAT ONE DREAMS, ALL DREAM.
IF SO, BELOVED, ALL WHO SLEPT SHOULD TRY TO REMEMBER. THE SHARED WISDOM OF THE DREAMS COULD BE VITAL.
HMM... COULD BE! SO WHO'S NEXT?
I AM!

NEWS OF REDLANCE'S DISTURBING DREAM GATHERS CURIOUS MEMBERS OF THE WOLFRIDER TRIBE IN THE HEART OF THORNY MOUNTAIN HOLT.
SPURRED BY THE VISION'S RETELLING, OTHERS LOOK DEEP -- INTO SHADOW PLACES WITHIN THEIR MINDS TO SEE IF CONNECTING IMAGES EMERGE.
WELL, PIKE, THIS IS YOUR SQUIRRELLY GAME. WHOSE NIGHTMARE GETS COUGHED UP NEXT?
IT'S GOOD TO LOOK FOR SOME MEANING... AFTER OUR LONG SLEEP UNDER-GROUND. I'LL TRY --
--UH UH, NIGHTFALL! SEEMS TO ME THE ONE WHO WAS IN REDLANCE'S DREAM SHOULD GO NEXT.
DREAMTIME PT. 2
HUH? THE ONE IN HIS DREAM?
TREE SPIRITS...? DEAD ELF SPIRITS...?
AW C'MON...! HUMANS?!

HEH HEH. NO, SKOT. DREAMS SOMETIMES PLAY WITH NAMES... TURN THEM INTO PICTURES.
REDLANCE SAW BURNT TREESTUMPS IN HIS DREAM!
IT'S TRUE! HE DID!
WELL, HANG ME RUMP SKYWARD!
¦SIGH¦ AWFUL WEIRD, PIKE! SO...?
SO-O-O...
"...WE SEND FOR TREESTUMP, ROCK-BRAIN!"
COCOONED TOGETHER FOR A MOUNTAIN'S AGE, OLD FRIEND, BUT I GUESS WE'RE BOTH STILL PRETTY SHARP! HEH HEH HEH...
DA DUMMM... DA DUMMM... DA DA DA FILLS THE NIGHT... FRIENDLY DARKNESS, WINKING ST--
WHURF!
KSHHIK
KSHHIK
KSHHIK
TREESTUMP!
TREESTUMP!
A COUNCIL!
HUH ?!
COMING!

MY DREAMS...?! OWL PELLETS! YOU HAULED MY TAIL HERE FOR THAT?!
CAN'T RECALL A CURSED THING--AND THAT'S JUST FINE WITH ME!
BUT--BUT THINK OF THE STORIES I COULD TELL!
COME ON! JUST TRY SOME DREAM-BERRIES--
--TO JOG YOUR MEMORY-- URRK!
AND ARE YOU THE ONE TO SHOVE 'EM DOWN MY GULLET IF I SAY NO?
UMM... UH... W-WELL...
HEH HEH... DREAMBERRIES WORKED FOR REDLANCE 'CAUSE HE'S FULL OF PLANT MAGIC.
M-MAYBE SOMETHING ELSE WILL SPARK YOUR--
--THE ONLY SPARKS YOU'LL SEE, MEDDLER, I'LL BE MAKING WITH MY SHARPSTONE!
UFF!
WHICH IS WHAT I WAS DOING WHEN YOU INTERRUPTED ME!
GRUMBLE ...GROWL ...RRRRRR
I'M WITH TREESTUMP, BELOVED. FINDING THE COMMON MESSAGE IN A BUNCH OF SLEEP-PICTURES--
--SEEMS AS SILLY AS TRYING TO PIN RAINDROPS TOGETHER WITH AN ARROW.
HMMM...

AND...
IS IT THAT YOU DON'T **WANT** TO REMEMBER, OLD FRIEND?
OH, LASS, IT WAS SO **SAD** WITHOUT YOU AND THE TWINS.
NOW WE'RE ALL TOGETHER AGAIN. WHY NOT JUST LIVE IN THE "NOW"?
KSHHIK
KSHHIK
HEY! YOU **DO** REMEMBER SOMETHING!
PLEASE... TELL US.

"REDLANCE DREAMT OUR BIRTH-HOLT WILL BE DESTROYED BY HUMANS... WITH GREAT BLADES MADE ALL OF METAL!"
"METAL WEAPONS IN HUMAN HANDS! TERRIBLE! BUT I-- I THINK I'VE SEEN EVEN WORSE."
"IN MY DREAM, I SEE MYSELF... AT LEAST THE GUARDIAN SPIRIT I THINK IS ME... BIG AS LIFE... NO, BIGGER... WIELDING AND WEARING THE SHINY STUFF."
"I BORROW ITS PROTECTIVE POWER... BECOME PART OF ITS MYSTERY."

"THE MYSTERY BEGINS WITH FIRE, THAT MUCH I KNOW. FROM GROUND TO MELTING POT... THEN TO COOL AIR AND HAMMER BLOWS."
"ALL THE MAKINGS OF THE WORLD ITSELF GO INTO THE FORGING OF A BLADE!"
"IT BEGINS IN FIRE AND FINISHES IN WATER. BUT THE BLADE ONLY LIVES -- REALLY LIVES -- WHEN MY HAND GRASPS IT!"

"HOW DO I USE THE SHARP, SHINING GIFT? I SERVE!"
"CUBS AND KIN... LIFEMATES AND CHIEFS... I GET BETWEEN THEM AND ALL THE DANGERS THERE ARE TO FACE."
"IT MAKES ME GLAD. IT'S ALL I WANT."

"TO FEED!"
"TO PROTECT!"

"AND I LOVE IT!"
"NOTHING CAN WITHSTAND THE KEEN EDGES OF MY TWO BLADES, THE STRENGTH IN MY TWO GOOD ARMS!"
"WHEN I SEE BLOOD FLOW, I THIRST FOR MORE!"
RRRAAAUUGH!!
"AND THERE IS ALWAYS MORE!"

"I'M AS STRONG AS MY SWORD... AS MIGHTY AS MY AXE... AS UNHURTABLE AS MY ARMOR!"
HA HA HA HAHAHA HA HA
HEYYOOOO!!!
"I SWING MY BLADES IN TRIUMPH, SLASHING THE AIR. THOSE I LOVE AND PROTECT HOWL FOR JOY!"
AYOOOAH!!
AYYOOOOAH!!
"NO FORCE CAN FELL ME--"

"--UNTIL... OH, HIGH ONES! THE TREES... THE TREES CLOSE IN!
"THE FOREST SHRINKS! NO ROOM FOR SLASHING!"
"BUT MY AXE! MY SWORD-- THEY SWING OUT OF CONTROL! HIGH ONES! CAN'T STOP!"
"WATCH OUT, CUBS! WATCH OUT!"
"CUBS!"

"NO...!"
"OH, NO......"

"THE WORLD'S GIFT, OUT OF CONTROL, HAS TAKEN MY DEAR ONES AWAY!"
"TEARS..."
"NOTHING COULD STOP THOSE COLD, SCREAMING BLADES."
"BUT MY TEARS WEAR THEM DOWN... TO NOTHING!"
"SO IT FINISHES IN WATER... A GREAT WAVE OF SALT TEARS... OVERWHELMING ALL!"

...THAT'S ALL I REMEMBER. AND I'LL NOT TELL IT AGAIN.
WE... UNDERSTAND.
WE'LL TELL IT FOR YOU, TREESTUMP. ANYWAY, I BET YOU HAD BETTER, HAPPIER DREAMS THAN THAT.
TRY TO REMEMBER THOSE.
AYE, CUB, BUT THIS IS THE ONE THAT STICKS. MAYBE PIKE CAN MAKE SOMETHING OF IT.
I'M JUST NOT SURE I WANT TO KNOW.
AND WHEN LEETAH HAS FAITHFULLY REPORTED TREESTUMP'S NIGHTMARE...
BELOVED, WE MUST CONTINUE!
AFTER ALL WE'VE BEEN THROUGH, WHY HAUNT OURSELVES WITH DARK MIND-STUFF THAT SHOULD STAY BURIED?
UM... CUTTER. I -- I DON'T MEAN TO SPEAK OUT OF TURN, BUT...
TREESTUMP'S DREAM... IT REMINDS ME. I'VE DREAMT OF BIG WAVES LIKE THAT SINCE I WAS A CHILD.
DID YOU SEE ONE WHILE WE SLEPT UNDERGROUND, ZHANTEE?
THAT... AND MORE. I'D LIKE TO TELL EVERYONE...
...IF IT'S ALL RIGHT, CUTTER...

TWO OF THE ELFIN TRIBE -- REDLANCE AND TREESTUMP -- HAVE TOLD OF THEIR NIGHTMARES, AND NOW PIKE'S DREAM-TEACHING GAME TAKES A DISTURBING TURN--
--ESPECIALLY FOR THE WOLFRIDERS' QUICK-TEMPERED CHIEF.
CUTTER...? IS IT ALL RIGHT IF I GO NEXT?
WHAT FOR, ZHANTEE? WE'VE A NEW HOLT TO SETTLE AND GAME TO HUNT--
--AND FOR THAT WE NEED OUR HEADS IN THE "NOW"-- EH ?!
SKYWISE! TIMMAIN BROUGHT YOU...?
DREAMTIME Pt 3
YEP! PICKED ME RIGHT UP FROM THE MOSS BED WHERE I WAS SNOOZING!
SHE "SENT" SOMETHING I DIDN'T QUITE CATCH. WHAT'S THIS ABOUT DREAMS?

ALL WHO SLEPT, WAITING TO REUNITE WITH YOU, ME AND THE TWINS --THEY ARE BEGINNING TO REMEMBER, SKYWISE.
AH! NOW THAT COULD MAKE FOR AN INTERESTING LISTEN --
GRUMPH!
--O-O-O-RRR... THEN AGAIN... MAYBE NOT!
WHAT...? WANT ME TO COME WITH YOU, HIGH ONE?
⦃SIGH⦄ ALL RIGHT... LET PIKE TAKE THOSE WHO WISH IT DOWN THE DARK DREAM PATH.
JUST DON'T COME BARKING TO ME IF SOMETHING BITES YOU ON THE WAY!
WHAT IN TIMMORN'S NAME DID YOU DREAM, OLDER BROTHER?
⦃WHEW⦄ UPSETTING HIM IS THE LAST THING I WANT!
MY BELOVED'S TEMPER IS AS IT ALWAYS WAS... ONLY MORE SO.
⦃GIGGLE⦄ THAT "MORE SO" EXTENDS TO OTHER THINGS, DOESN'T IT, SISTER?
⦃AHEM!⦄ WELL, ZHANTEE YOU HEARD HIM GO ON! TELL US YOUR DREAM!

LESS EAGER THAN BEFORE, ZHANTEE WALKS THOUGHTFULLY... SILENTLY... FOLLOWED BY THOSE WITH WHOM HE FEELS THE MOST KINSHIP.
ARRIVING AT THE BARE SEA CLIFFS BEYOND THE FOREST'S EDGE, THE ELVES GAZE AT THE ROCK-BOUND SHORE OF THEIR NEW LAND.
BENEATH THE WAVES, WHERE THE WATER IS STILL, THE PALACE OF THE HIGH ONES LIES RESTING.
I MISS IT... MISS THE FEELING OF REALLY FLYING.
SOMEDAY MY SIRE, RAYEK, WILL RAISE IT FROM THE DEPTHS.
I KNOW HE WILL, VENKA! HE'LL MEET THE CHALLENGE.
BUT TILL THEN, WE MUST FLY IN OUR DREAMS.
ALL OF YOU... EVEN PIKE... YOU'RE THE ONLY ONES WHO CAN UNDERSTAND. I'M NOT REALLY A WOLFRIDER.
MY DREAM ISN'T DARK, LIKE REDLANCE'S OR TREESTUMP'S. NOTHING HINDERED ME. NOTHING I LOVED DIED.
CUTTER MIGHT TAKE OFFENSE--
--BECAUSE YOU SAW ONLY VISIONS OF LIGHT?! DON'T BE SILLY! GO ON!

"BUT I AM SILLY, HEALER... ALWAYS HAVE BEEN! PLACID AND SOFT AS THE ROLLING DUNES :HEH HEH...: "
"IN MY SLEEP I SEE THEM OVER AND OVER AGAIN, THE DUNES... AS IF THE SUN IS MY HOME AND I LOOK DOWN ON THEM FROM HIGH IN THE BLAZING SKY."
"I SEE SORROW'S END TOO, OUR VILLAGE AND OUR FOLK. IT SEEMS I SWOOP DOWN TO THEM LIKE A DESERT HAWK ON THE WING."

"BUT, ONCE INSIDE THE VILLAGE, I SEE IT AS A CHILD WOULD... THE HUTS TOWERING ABOVE MY HEAD..."
"... AND THE SURROUNDING MOUNTAINS, MUCH MUCH TALLER THAN THE HUTS."
"YET NOTHING LOOMS AND INVITES LIKE THE BRIDGE OF DESTINY!"
"MOTHER, FATHER, THE RULING VOICES OF MY CHILDHOOD WARN, 'BE CAREFUL! DON'T GO UP THERE!'"
"MUSN'T TAKE RISKS, LITTLE ONE, MUSN'T TRY TO TOUCH THE SKY!"
"A GREAT 'NO' BARS MY WAY, RINGS IN MY DREAM-EARS. I FEEL HEAVY... ROOTED TO THE SPOT."

" THEN, FROM BEHIND THE BIG 'NO', WHO DO YOU SUPPOSE BECKONS ... ? RAYEK ! "
" KNOWING THAT I LONG TO BE AS DARING AS HE, HE POINTS ME TOWARD THE FORBIDDEN HEIGHTS. "
" BUT, AS HE DOES, THE MOUNTAINS DISSOLVE ! THE DESERT SANDS BEGIN TO ROLL AND HEAVE ! "
" THEY CHANGE, BECOMING TRANSPARENT AS GREEN CLEARSTONE, RISING HIGHER AND HIGHER AGAINST THE BRIGHTEST OF ALL SKIES ! "

"WATER... THE DESERT HAS TURNED ENTIRELY TO WATER! A SINGLE, ARCHING WAVE GATHERS FORCE AS IT RUSHES, HUGE BEYOND BELIEF, TOWARD SORROW'S END..."
"...TOWARD ME! I DON'T EVEN TRY TO RUN. IT'S NO USE. THERE'S NO ESCAPE FOR THE VILLAGE OR ANYONE IN IT."
"I KNOW, BECAUSE I'VE SEEN THIS WAVE BEFORE... STOOD AND LET IT WASH OVER ME BEFORE... AS IT DOES NOW."

"AND JUST LIKE ALL THE OTHER TIMES, I'M NOT AFRAID."
--NO! THE REAL SEA FEELS... REAL! PAINFULLY SO!
BUT NONE OF US SUN FOLK EVER SAW THE VASTDEEP WATER, UNTIL NOW.
JUST DAYS AGO YOU SAVED ME... SHIELDED ME FROM SUCH A WAVE. PERHAPS THAT COLORS HOW YOU RECALL --?
BUT NEVER, IN MY SLEEP, ARE THERE THE DEADLY ROCKS OR NUMBING COLD.
THE DREAM-WAVE TUMBLES ME, BUT I CAN STILL BREATHE. IT'S NOT UNPLEASANT AT ALL.
HMMM... MUST BE A SYMBOL, THEN?
SOMEDAY I'LL KNOW WHAT IT MEANS.
IS THERE MORE?
MORE, SHENSHEN? ;CHUCKLE; WELL, YES... IF YOUR SISTER WILL PARDON ME!
PART OF MY DREAM, AT LEAST, HAS COME TRUE SINCE OUR AWAKENING. NO MATTER HOW DEEP I PLUNGE, MY SHIELD PROTECTS ME.
BREATHING UNDER WATER IS LIKE FLYING, ONLY BETTER. HOW COULD EVEN WINNOWILL STAY SO BAD, WHEN IT FEELS SO WONDERFUL?

"AFTER THE DREAM-WAVE HITS, THE SUN VILLAGE IS FORGOTTEN. I KNOW THE OTHERS ARE LIKE ME NOW -- WEIGHTLESS, TIRELESS, LACKING NOTHING, FULL OF JOY."
"BUT THEN, LOOKING UP THROUGH THE BOTTOMLESS GREEN, I SEE A SHINING BALL -- THE DAYSTAR -- THE SUN!"
"AND I REALIZE I STILL WANT SOMETHING... SOMETHING I KNOW IS THERE, ABOVE."
"SO I SWIM TOWARD IT..."
"...AND FIND WHAT I SEEK..."

"YOU, LEETAH. YOU ARE THE SUN!"

"WITH ONE WARM, GENTLE HAND, YOU DRAW ME OUT OF THE WATER... AND WITH THE OTHER YOU POINT THE WAY TO THE PALACE."
"YOU CHALLENGE ME TO KEEP GOING, EVEN THOUGH I WANT VERY MUCH TO STAY."
"FOR A MOMENT-- WE COME SO CLOSE--"

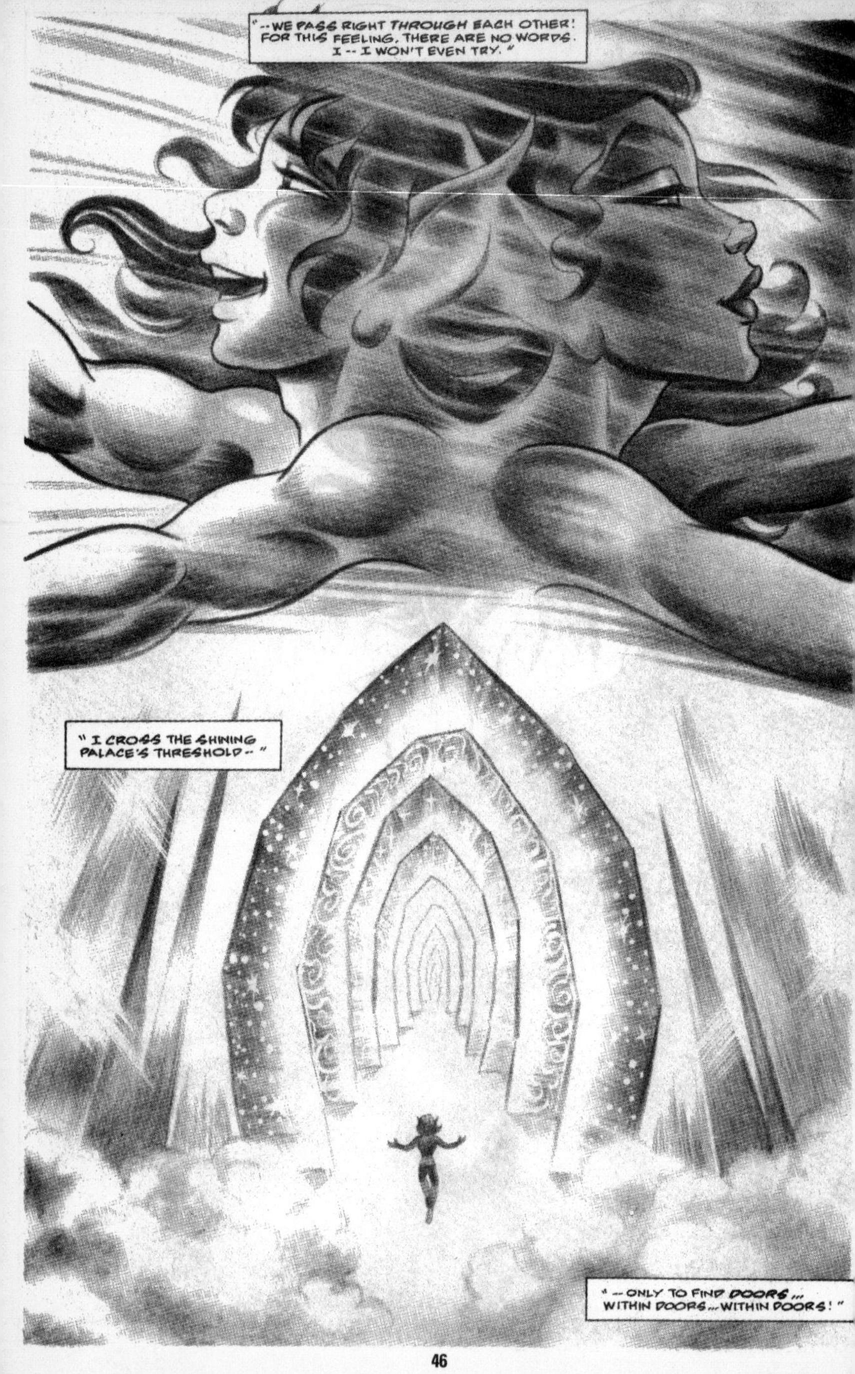
"--WE PASS RIGHT THROUGH EACH OTHER! FOR THIS FEELING, THERE ARE NO WORDS. I -- I WON'T EVEN TRY."
"I CROSS THE SHINING PALACE'S THRESHOLD--"
"--ONLY TO FIND DOORS... WITHIN DOORS... WITHIN DOORS!"

IT SEEMS EACH ONE OPENS ON SUCH A BIG ADVENTURE, I DON'T EVER WANT TO TURN BACK!
YOU CAN ALL LAUGH NOW. IT IS A BIG-HEADED VISION FOR AN ELF LIKE ME.
I'M STILL NOT SURE WHY TIMMAIN CHOSE ME TO BE PART OF CUTTER'S BAND.
SURELY SHE SENSED THE POWER THAT SLEPT WITHIN YOU... THE POWER TO SHIELD OTHERS FROM HARM.
SHE KNEW, DESPITE YOUR SHYNESS, YOU'D BE ABLE TO KEEP UP WITH THE WOLFRIDERS...
"... AND THAT, COME WHAT MAY, YOU'D ALWAYS PUT THEIR NEEDS BEFORE YOUR OWN."
OH... I'M NOT SO NOBLE! IT'S JUST... THE WOLF-RIDERS MAKE THINGS HAPPEN... THINGS THAT MAKE ME STRETCH.
THOUGH OUR CHIEF'S GROWLS STILL UNNERVE ME, I GUESS I LIKE FACING ALL THE TESTS.
AND WHAT MORE THAN THAT DOES IT TAKE TO BE A TRUE WOLFRIDER?

YOU SAVED THE SUN THAT LIGHTS UP BOTH OUR LIVES.
SO WHAT'S THE IDEA OF EVEN QUESTIONING TIMMAIN'S CHOICE?
SNIFF
WHEN THIS GAME IS DONE, AND ALL THOSE PRECIOUS DREAM-STORIES ARE STRUNG TO-GETHER --
-- WE NEED A SAFER PLACE THAN MY NUTSHELL OF A HEAD TO KEEP THEM!
PERHAPS THE SCROLL OF COLORS RECORDS WHAT WE DREAM, AS WELL AS WHAT WE DO.
MY FATHER MIGHT KNOW. IT'S TIME I RETURN TO HIM.
ZHANTEE, BEFORE YOU GO BACK -- PLEASE TAKE ME TO RAYEK!

ANOTHER DAWN APPROACHES ON THE WORLD OF TWO MOONS ...
YET THE GENTLE GLOW THAT SUFFUSES THE COASTAL WATERS COMES NOT FROM THE SKY ABOVE, BUT FROM THE AURA SURROUNDING THE SUNKEN PALACE OF THE HIGH ONES.
AS A MAGICALLY SHIELDED ZHANTEE BEARS VENKA TO THE CRYSTALLINE STRUCTURE'S PORTAL ...
HEARING YOUR DREAM HELPED ME RECALL BITS OF MY OWN, LOVEMATE. FOR ME, THAT IS UNUSUAL.
I'M GLAD PIKE STARTED HIS DREAM-SHARING GAME.
ELSE I'D NEVER HAVE HAD THE NERVE TO TELL LEETAH HOW I --
DREAMTIME PATH

HEH HEH HEH
I WOULDN'T WORRY. EVEN THE WOLVES KNOW HOW MUCH YOU MISSED HER.
AH! THERE'S FAITHFUL EKUAR... WAVING FROM THE DOOR.
MY LONELY SIRE IS FORTUNATE TO HAVE HIS COMPANY JUST NOW.
ZHANTEE DIVES FOR THE SHIMMERING DOORWAY AND --
--PIERCES THE MEMBRANE WHICH HOLDS BACK THE MIGHTY, SALT FLOOD.
WELCOME, CHILDREN, WELCOME! MIND THAT SLIPPERY FLOOR, NOW!
SIGH
EACH ENTRY INTO THE PALACE IS AS WONDROUS AS THE FIRST!
WITHIN, MUSICAL CHATTER ECHOES...
ARE THE WOLFRIDERS WELL, DEAR VENKA? GROWING ACCUS-TOMED TO THE WORLD'S MANY CHANGES?
YES. SLOWLY. REDLANCE IS RE-SHAPING OUR LONG OVERGROWN HOLT FROM THE BARE SOIL UP.
YOUNG ZHANTEE! WILL YOU NOT STAY AND VISIT?
SURELY... WHEN I RETURN WITH MORE SUPPLIES!
THANK YOU, LOVEMATE.
EKUAR... HOW IS...?
CLOSER TO DESPAIR THAN I'VE EVER SEEN HIM.
THE POWER TO MAKE THE PALACE FLY MEANT EVERYTHING TO POOR BROWNSKIN-- AND NOT JUST FOR SHOW.
HE TRULY INTENDED TO HELP THIS WORLD'S ELVES REGAIN THE GLORY OF THE HIGH ONES.
YET EVEN WHEN TIMMAIN, THE LIVING HIGH ONE, WOULD NOT SUPPORT HIS PLAN, HE REFUSED TO HEAR... TO SEE.
ONLY THE THOUGHT OF LOSING YOU GAVE HIM PAUSE AT LAST.

MOMENTS LATER...
DRIFTING... FLOATING... BUT NO VOLUNTARY MOVEMENT... NO TRACE OF EXPRESSION.
RAYEK...?
:AHEM: FATHER...?
YOU CANNOT KNOW WHAT A SHAME THIS IS, VENKA. WINNOWILL HAS BEEN MANY THINGS...
...BUT, ABOVE ALL, SHE WAS A CREATURE OF FIERCE AND FORCEFUL LIFE.
WHEN WILL SHE COME BACK TO ME?
I'VE A QUESTION FOR YOU.
DOES THE SCROLL OF COLORS RECORD DREAMS AS WELL AS DEEDS?

SIGH
THAT I CANNOT TELL YOU.
YOU SEE... I'VE LOST THE POWER TO TURN THE SCROLL.
WHY DO YOU ASK?

WHILE WE SLEPT IN COCOONS OF PRESERVER WEBBING, OUR MINDS WERE NOT ALWAYS STILL.
PIKE IS COLLECTING OUR DREAMS. HE THINKS A COMMON THREAD BINDS THEM.
I THOUGHT, PERHAPS, BY READING THE SCROLL, WE MIGHT QUICKLY DISCOVER THAT THREAD AND THE WISDOM WOVEN THROUGH IT.
I DON'T UNDERSTAND...

HOW DID HE DO IT? HOW DID CUTTER CONVINCE ALL OF YOU TO SLEEP A GREAT PORTION OF YOUR LIVES AWAY... FOR HIS SAKE?
HE DID NOT. WE OFFERED.
WE LOVE HIM, YOU SEE.

THERE IS NO DIFFERENCE BETWEEN THE "NOW OF WOLF THOUGHT" AND IMMORTALITY.
IN EITHER STATE THE SENSE OF PASSING TIME IS ABSENT...
...EXCEPT FOR CUTTER.

HE ALONE FELT EACH DAY'S LOSS AS HE WAITED TO FIND HIS FAMILY AGAIN. FINALLY, HE COULD NO LONGER BEAR IT.
ALL HE EVER ASKED IS THAT WE FOLLOW HIM FREELY.
"WE DID. IT WAS THE LEAST WE COULD DO."
"THERE WAS NOTHING TO DREAD. THE TROLLS, PRESERVERS AND TIMMAIN WATCHED OVER US AND THE WOLF PACK AS WE SLEPT."
"SOMETIMES, WHEN OUR SOULS WERE NOT ADRIFT IN THE WORLD OF DREAMS, WE EVEN SENT TO EACH OTHER."
SO YOU SEE, IF SACRIFICE THERE WAS, IT WAS NOT SO TERRIBLE.
WHAT DID YOU DREAM?

HMMM... IT'S NOT SO EASY TO SORT VAGUE MEMORIES FROM SLEEP-VISIONS.
BUT I DO RECALL MY OLDEST NIGHT-MARE... BRIEF... EVER REPEATING.
"FIRST I HEAR SOUNDS, LIKE BRITTLE THUNDER, CRASHING AND SMASHING OUTSIDE."
"THEN, WITH AN INFANT'S EYES I SEE A TERRIBLE THREAT FROM ABOVE."
"MY TINY HAMMOCK ROCKS WILDLY. BITS OF WOOD AND CLAY AND JAGGED STONE RAIN DOWN ON ME, STRIKE ME..."
"...AND, THOUGH I SCREAM FOR MY VERY LIFE, NO ONE COMES TO MY AID!"
"THAT'S ALL. IT SEEMS VERY REAL. BUT..."

I -- I THOUGHT YOU WERE DEAD! YOUR CURSED MOTHER, KAHVI, TOLD ME SO!
SO IT WAS YOU WHO ATTACKED THE LODGE... WITH ME IN IT!
BY THE DAYSTAR! IS THERE NO END TO MY ERRORS?!
VENKA...
IT'S ALL RIGHT. I DON'T THINK I'LL EVER HAVE THAT BAD DREAM AGAIN.
YOUR HATRED OF KAHVI... YOUR BANISHMENT OF THE GO-BACKS... ODD... SO ODD!
THESE THINGS ARE FRESH IN YOUR MIND. BUT I CAN ONLY DIMLY RECALL MY MOTHER'S FACE...
...IN MY OWN REFLECTION.
"IN TRUTH, SHE IS BUT HALF OF ME... THAT BOLD WARRIOR OF THE FROZEN MOUNTAINS. NOT FROM HER BREAST COMES WARMTH AND AFFECTION, FOR IT IS ENCASED IN BITTER, COLD ARMOR."
"THE WARMTH I FIND IN MY OTHER HALF, THE HALF BORN OF THE DESERT. FIRES OF WISDOM AND INNER POWER BURN STEADILY, CONTAINED AND USEFUL."

"IN MY DREAM, THE MOTHER OF MEMORY REACHES OUT TO ME AND I REACH BACK."
"GENTLY, BUT FIRMLY, SHE PUSHES ASIDE THE HOWLING BERSERKER WHO WOULD FREEZE MY HEART AND USE ME AS HER TOOL OF VENGEANCE."
"WE TOUCH. I AM GOWNED LIKE HER ... CALM LIKE HER. WISDOM POURS INTO MY SOUL, ENDLESSLY, LIKE THE RAYS OF THE SUN."
"WE STAND ATOP A PLACE I KNOW TO BE THE BRIDGE OF DESTINY. IT IS MADE ALL OF FLAMES THAT LAP AT MY ANKLES ... BUT DO NOT BURN."

"THEN I HEAR MY MOTHER'S VOICE CALLING MY NAME. A FROSTY WIND CHILLS MY SPINE."
"HOW HEROIC SHE IS... HOW DETERMINED! NOW I AM DRAWN TO HER. SHE HAS LEARNED HOW TO GET WHAT SHE WANTS FROM ME."
"I TURN TO MEET KAHVI'S STARE. WHERE HER FEET TOUCH THE FIERY BRIDGE, ICE FORMS, FLOWING DOWN TO SNOW-CAPPED PEAKS."
"BEHIND HER, MISTY FIGURES -- THEY MUST BE GO-BACKS -- SEEM EAGER, ANTICIPATING HER NEXT MOVE."
"MOTHER HANDS ME HER SWORD AND SHIELD..."

"... AND I, DELICATELY CLAD AS ANY MILD SUN VILLAGER, RISE ALOFT WITH THEM FROM THE BRIDGE!"
"THE SHIELD, MINE TO CARRY WHEREVER I GO, IS WEIGHT LESS, ABLAZE WITH LIGHT, ITS PROTECTION UNDENIABL
"THE SWORD, NO MORE BURDENSOME THAN THE SHIELD, IS A TRANSPARENT SHARD OF ICE, CLEAR AND COOL AS REASON ITSELF."
"THUS ARMED, I RISE ABOVE THE CHEERING GO-BACKS -- WHO REVEAL WOLFRIDERS, TOO, AMONG THEIR RANKS."

I ONLY HOPE THAT MEETING ME... HAS PLACED NO CONFLICT IN YOUR HEART.
MEETING YOU HAS **RESOLVED** IT.

SHORTLY, IN THORNY MOUNTAIN HOLT...
THAT VENKA IS A POWERFUL SENDER... ALL THE WAY FROM UNDER THE SEA!
INTERESTING DREAM TOO!
WE'VE RAISED HER AS ONE OF US, BUT SHE'S NEVER BEEN QUITE LIKE US.
AND YET SHE'S MORE A WOLFRIDER THAN SHE THINKS.
WHAT, BELOVED?
NOTHING. YOU KNOW.
AND ONLY YOU, FOR I'VE TOLD NO ONE ELSE HOW KAHVI INTERRUPTED MY LONG SLUMBER...
...NOT YET.
THE SUN IS UP, TRIBEMATES, OR HADN'T YOU NOTICED?
TIME TO LAY ASIDE PIKE'S IDLE GAME AND GET SOME SIMPLE, PRACTICAL REST.
HOPEFULLY WITHOUT ANY DREAMS FOR ONCE!

REDLANCE... NIGHTFALL...
WILL YOU "TREE" WITH US TODAY?
OH...! WE WOULDN'T THINK OF INTRUDING, LEETAH!
YOU AND CUTTER HAVE BEEN REUNITED SUCH A SHORT WHILE...
HEY! YOU'RE MY FAMILY TOO.
AND MINE. PLEASE COME WITH US.
HO HUM! I GUESS THE FURS ARE CALLING...
AND...
LOOK AT HIM! CUTTER FLIES FROM BRANCH TO BRANCH AS MERRILY AS A PRESERVER!
HA HA HAH! ARE YOU THAT SLEEPY? YOU CLIMB LIKE BABY TREEWEES!
CREAK!
SKSSHH!

BUT, AS THE DROWSY DAY PASSES, NOTHING CAN LONG STAY HIDDEN AMONG LOVING FRIENDS...

SO THE GO-BACKS CARRY A DROP OF WOLF BLOOD FROM TWO-SPEAR'S TIME! A DROP SO THIN, NONE OF US COULD SCENT IT!

HOW CAN I THANK YOU, NIGHTFALL? YOU SHIELDED CUTTER FROM KAHVI'S GREED EVEN AS I WOULD.

DON'T THINK TWICE OF IT. I DIDN'T.

LIFEMATE... LOVEMATES... TRIBEMATES... YOU'RE ALL ONE TO ME. THERE'S NOTHING I WOULDN'T DO FOR YOU...

PEACEFUL EVENING - DAYBREAK TO THE NOCTURNAL WOLFRIDERS - DESCENDS ON THORNY MOUNTAIN HOLT...
NIGHTFALL AND REDLANCE'S GENTLE DAUGHTER, ARISEN WELL BEFORE HER PARENTS, LOOKS AFTER THE TRIBE'S YOUNGEST MEMBERS.
SEE, TYLEET? THE MOONHATCHERS! THEY'RE FINALLY HERE!
WAAK WAAAK WAK WAK
SO TINY! SO BRAVE! LISTEN TO THEIR MOTHER CALL THEM!
OH-OH-OH! LOOK! THE FIRST ONE'S GETTING READY TO JUMP!
DREAMTIME Pt 5
SHHH, EMBER! DON'T FRIGHTEN THEM!
AH... A RARE SIGHT!

PEEP PEEP PEEP PEEP PEEP
"COURAGE IS BORN IN THOSE LITTLE ONES, TO MAKE THAT FIRST, TERRIBLE LEAP UNAIDED!"
AYOOOAH!!
GOOD JUMP!
KWOK KWOK KWOK
PLUNK!
FOUR... FIVE...SIX... Whew! THEY ALL MADE IT!
PLOPP!
KERPLUNK!
YES, SUNTOP! A HARD WAY TO BEGIN LIFE, ISN'T IT?
BUT THEIR MOTHER'S PROUD! THEY'VE PROVED THEY'RE STRONG!
SPLOOSH!
PEEP PEEP PEEP PEEP
A MOTHER IS ALWAYS PROUD OF HER YOUNG.
BE THEY HELPLESS AT BIRTH OR NO, SHE'LL GUARD THEM WITH HER LIFE--

--UNTIL THEY'RE
LONGER CHILDREN.
UNTIL THEY'RE
BIG ENOUGH
BE CALLED
FRIENDS!
NEVER
TOO BIG TO
CUDDLE UNDER
MOTHER'S WING
NOW AND
THEN!

TIME
TO GO!
OOOWWWOOOOOOOOO!

SWIFTLY, NIGHTFALL'S CHOSEN HUNTING PARTNERS RESPOND TO HER CALL.

Pant Pant Pant
WHUFF!

PHEW!! THAT'S WORSE THAN USUAL!

WHAT IN TIMMORN'S NAME HAVE YOU BEEN ROLLING IN?!

WHO, NIGHTFALL?

YOUR WOLF-FRIEND?

OR ME?

Sniff Sniff

I'M NOT SO SURE, PIKE!

OH, WELL... WE'LL ALL SMELL ALIKE SOON ENOUGH!

Heh Heh Heh...

YOU'VE GOT THAT RIGHT!

LET'S GO!

YOU KNOW...
...YOU NEVER GOT AROUND TO TELLING ME YOUR DREAM.
SO, YOU'VE FINALLY DECIDED IT'S MY TURN, EH?
SORRY...
...NO!
YOU GAVE ME TIME TO PONDER.
NOW THAT I'VE HEARD SOME OF THE OTHERS' DREAMS, I SEE WHERE MINE FITS IN.
"IN MY SLEEP I OFTEN RELIVED THOSE HAPPY DAYS WHEN TYLEET AND VENKA WERE LITTLE CUBS."
"MY DREAM-HOLT SEEMS MORE THAN BEAUTIFUL, THE TREES TALLER, THE FLOWERS BRIGHTER..."
"...THOUGH NOT SO BRIGHT AS MY DEAR ONES' SMILES."
"THEN... REDLANCE COMES TO ME, BEARING A SINGLE, SAD, WITHERED FLOWER IN HIS HANDS."
"HE BEGINS TO WORK HIS TREE-SHAPING MAGIC..."

"...AND SOON THE FLOWER BLOOMS AGAIN, GROWING AND GROWING..."
"...UNTIL, NURTURED BY ALL OUR LOVE, IT TAKES FORM..."
"...AS CUTTER!"
"HIS RENEWED POWER SPEARS THROUGH THE HOLT LIKE PAINLESS SKYFIRE, GIVING VIGOR TO ALL LIVING THINGS--UNITING US ALL IN THE WAY."
"AS OUR CHIEF THRIVES, SO THRIVES THE TRIBE..."

"...AND WE KNOW THE JOY OF AIDING HIM, AS FRIENDS OF HIS BODY AND SPIRIT!"
"BUT THEN..."
"...A DARK SHADOW SLINKS FROM THE FOREST. IT'S COME TO DIM THE LIGHT OF OUR PEACE!"
"I KNOW THIS SHADOW. IT HUNGERS FOR WHAT WE HAVE."
"AND IT HAS NO EYES TO SEE THE DREADFUL HARM IT WILL WREAK AS IT SATISFIES ITS NEED."
"THE COLD, GREEDY SHADE FEEDS ON CUTTER'S STRENGTH, DRAWING HIM IN..."
"...AWAY FROM US!"

"I SEE THE FOREST FADING, THE WAY FADING..."
"...CUBS, CHIEF AND LIFEMATE ALL CONSUMED BY THAT RAVENOUS SHADOW!"
"NO! NOT WHILE MY STEADY ARM CAN STILL FIRE ONE CLEAN SHOT!"
"MY ARROW TEARS THE DARK THING AT ITS CORE!"
"BUT THERE IS NO DEATH SCREAM. WHAT I HEAR..."
S LAUGHTER."
"THE SHREDS OF SHADOW WRITHE AND RE-FORM. AND I RECOGNIZE THESE SHAPES TOO."
HA HA HA HA HA HA
"THESE ARE THE USERS AMONG OUR OWN KIND... THE LOVELESS ONES..."

"...WITHOUT PITY..."
"...WITHOUT LOYALTY..."
"...WITHOUT REGARD FOR THE HOPES AND WISHES OF ANY BUT THEMSELVES."
"WITH THESE SHADOW MEMBERS OF OUR RACE BEGINS THE HOLT'S DOWNFALL!"
HA HA
"NO OTHERS ARE TO BLAME! THE FAULT IS OURS!"
HA HA
HA
"YET I'LL FIGHT THEM TO THE LAST, PIERCE THEIR DARKNESS THREE TIMES OVER TO SAVE WHAT I LOVE MOST!"

"THREE ARROWS FLY!"
"AND ALL THREE FIND THEIR MARK!"
"WOUNDED, THE DARK ONES RETREAT WITH WHAT'S LEFT OF MY FAMILY AND VENKA!"
"AND BARRING MY PATH, A CROWD OF HUMANS APPEARS... FEEDING LIKE CARRION BIRDS ON THE LAST, LIFE-DRAINED TWIGS OF MY HOME!"
"I WON'T GIVE UP!"
"I GIVE CHASE, RIGHT THROUGH THAT WALL OF SCAVENGING HUMANS..."
"...INTO THE DEEPEST, COLDEST EMPTINESS I'VE EVER KNOWN!"

"REDLANCE...!"
"CUTTER...!"
"CUBS!"
"NOW I'M IN THE GO-BACKS' LODGE, FACING THE LOVELESS ONES WHO'VE RESTORED THEMSELVES BY FEEDING ON THEIR CAPTIVES' SPIRITS!"
"THIS IS THE PLACE WHERE REDLANCE FOUGHT ALONE, DURING THE PALACE WAR BECAUSE I COULDN'T BE THERE TO HELP HIM!"
"WELL, I'M HERE NOW...!"

"AND FOR WHAT THEY'VE DONE TO MY LIFEMATE, WHO IS THE HOLT..."
"...TO CUTTER, WHO IS THE WAY..."
"...AND TO THE PRECIOUS CUBS WHO ARE OUR TRIBE'S ONE PROMISE OF SURVIVAL..."
"...I WILL TAKE TERRIBLE REVENGE!"
"WINNOWILL...!"
"RAYEK...!"
"TWO EDGE...!"
"AND YOU, HUNGRY, LURKING SHADOW...!"

"I'LL DESTROY YOU ALL!"
"MY QUIVER IS BOTTOMLESS... MY ARROWS A PIERCING HAIL!"
HA HA
HA HA
"BUT THE INFURIATING LAUGHTER GOES ON!"
HA HA
HA HA HA
"THE SHADOWS ONLY GROW LARGER AS THEIR CAPTIVES SHRIVEL, ALMOST TO NOTHING!"
"HOW CAN I SAVE THEIR LIVES?! HOW?!!"

"THEN... THE ANSWER COMES, CLEAR AS MORNING DEWDROPS. WHY DIDN'T I THINK OF IT BEFORE?!"
"JUST AS TRIUMPH SEEMS WITHIN MY GRASP..."
"...EVERYTHING VANISHES! AND I FORGET WHAT IT WAS I MIGHT HAVE DONE TO SAVE MY DEAR ONES!"
"THAT WAS THE MOMENT KAHVI, MISTAKING ME FOR CUTTER, SLICED OPEN MY COCOON --"
--AND WOKE ME. I THINK SHE HERSELF CAUSED MY DREAM.
SOMEHOW... I MUST HAVE SENSED HER COMING.
Wheeeew!
SCARY! NONE OF US, NOT EVEN STRONGBOW, HAS EVER OUTMATCHED YOUR WILL TO PROTECT.
DO YOU SEE, NOW, HOW MY DREAM FITS IN... AT LEAST WITH REDLANCE'S AND TREESTUMP'S?
Hmmm... I GUESS WE PURE-BLOODED WOLFRIDERS CAN'T HELP BUT SHARE THE SAME WORRIES.
STILL, THERE'S MORE TO IT THAN THAT, OR THERE'S NO FIGURING MY DREAM IN!
WAIT'LL YOU HEAR-- Eh?!
Sniff Sniff
NIGHTFALL... JUST BEYOND THOSE BUSHES! A TUSK-HOG!
Whuff

HEY! WHERE ARE ***YOU*** GOING?
IT'S... JUST NOT IN ME TO KILL TONIGHT, PIKE. SORRY.
DON'T TAKE ON THAT TUSK-HOG ALONE. SEND FOR THE OTHERS.
Hmph!

THERE IS A SACRED PACT BETWEEN HUNTER AND PREY. BOTH MUST BE UP FOR THE HUNT, OR IT'S NO GOOD.
BUT THERE ARE THOSE, LIKE THE MOON HATCHERS, WHO ***CAN*** USE AND THROW RARE THINGS AWAY WITHOUT CARING.

MOTHER! BACK SO SOON?
giggle! TICKLES, HUH, EMBER?
KWOK
KWOK
KWOK

THERE'S A TIME TO ***KILL***... AND A TIME TO SIT AND WATCH--

--THE BEAUTY WE SOMETIMES FORGET TO SEE...

JUST PAST A TANGLE OF BUSHES, ONE OF **THORNY MOUNTAIN HOLT'S** MOST ***VICIOUS*** DENIZENS ROOTS FOR GRUBS...
Humph! ***NIGHTFALL*** MUST THINK FACE FUR MEANS NOTHING MORE THAN A WARM CHIN!
"DON'T TAKE ON THAT TUSK-HOG ALONE, PIKE."
RUNK RUNK RUNK
I'LL SHOW 'ER! I'LL CATCH IT WITH MY ***BARE HANDS!***
CHONK!
whi-i-i-ine...?
COME ON, TREMBLY BONES, DON'T BE SUCH A RABBIT!

RUNK RUNK
FOOF
RUNK RUNK RUNK
GOTCHA!
REEEEEEEEEEE!!
WOA!
RRRURRH!
WHOA!
RREEEUUURR!
I SAID WHOA!
SNORT
WOOPFF!!
SNORT SNORT!

OOF!
UFF!
OOF!
HRRRRUUUURRR!

Whine Whine
DON'T WORRY...!
I GOT 'IM
Unh --

--RIGHT WHERE
oopf
I WANT 'IM
unh!
SNORT SNORT SNORT

GASP!!!

YAAAH!

SSSKSSSHHH!!

EEYOWFF!
BAP!
RRRRRRRH!

UUNH!!
AUGH!!
KLUDD!!

???
YOU ROCK-BRAIN! THAT ROOT COULD'VE BUSTED YOUR TAIL!
WHERE'S YOUR SPEAR?! AND WHY WERE YOU HUNTING ALONE?

I HAD 'IM, CUTTER, 'TIL YOU CAME ALONG!
SURE YOU DID!
TUSK-HOGS AREN'T SO TOUGH TO CATCH. YOU JUST GOTTA THINK LIKE 'EM!

FOR YOU THAT SHOULD BE EASY!
COME ON! I'LL SHOW YOU HOW TO SNAG ONE WITHOUT A WEAPON!
Sniff snuffle

sniff sniff
HMMM... HE WENT THAT WAY. BUT LET ME MAKE THE CATCH.
I WANT TO PROVE TO NIGHTFALL IT CAN BE DONE SINGLE-HANDED!

THIS I MUST SEE!
HER DREAM WAS A REAL FOOT-FLAILER, BY THE WAY...
...FULL OF THREATS AND DANGER TO FAMILY AND HOLT.

SOUNDS BAD AS BEING AWAKE!
UH-UH. THERE WAS HOPE. HER DREAM WAS TRYING TO SHOW HER HOW TO WIN...
...BUT KAHVI WOKE HER BEFORE IT COULD.

DREAMS NEVER MEAN ANYTHING... NEVER SOLVE ANYTHING.

YOU DON'T BELIEVE THAT. AND I SURE DON'T--
--NOT AFTER THE ONE I HAD!

"JUST PICTURE IT...! THE TROLLS HAVE BROUGHT A GREAT VAT OF DREAMBERRIES INTO THE HOLT! EVERYBODY'S SILLY ON FRESH-TROMPED WINE!"
"I'M DANCING IN THE VAT WITH SOME HALF-CLOTHED TROLL LOVELIES... SQUISHING THE BERRIES WITH MY FEET... FEELING THE JUICE RUNNING BETWEEN MY TOES!"
"WE'RE ALL LAUGHING AND SINGING! IT'S A GUZZLE-NUZZLE PARTY!"
"}snerk{ I'VE SWALLOWED SO MANY CRUSHED BERRIES--"
"--EVEN THE TROLL MAIDENS LOOK BEAUTIFUL TO ME!"
"THAT IS, 'TIL ALL THE HUGGING AND LIP-SMUSHING STARTS!"
"YOUCH! I'M BEING SQUOOSHED LIKE A DREAMBERRY!"

snort WHAT A PREDICAMENT!
SHH!
SMELL 'IM? TUSK-HOG'S GONE TO GROUND --RIGHT THERE!
ALL WE HAVE TO DO IS LURE 'IM OUT.
SO... STICK YOUR RUMP IN THE MOUTH OF HIS DEN. SEE WHAT HAPPENS.

"WELL, THEY'RE SMOTHERING ME, YOU KNOW? AND THE TRIBE'S NO HELP... BUNCH OF HOWLING HOOT OWLS!"
"I HAVE TO ESCAPE. BUT HOW?"
"SEEMS LIKE THE ONLY WAY IS TO GET... SMALLER!"
"SO I DO JUST THAT! SMALLER..."
"...AND SMALLER..."
"...'TIL, AT LAST, I WRIGGLE FREE OF THE TROLL MAIDENS' CLUTCHES..."
"...AND SINK DOWN AMONG ALL THOSE LUSCIOUS BERRIES! YUMMM!"
"HIDING THERE, I KNOW I'M SAFE."
"BUT NO! THEY COME DIGGING FOR ME!"
"AT MY SIZE, IF THEIR BIG, FAT PAWS GRAB ME--"
RRRR....UUUURRR....
--THEY'LL POP MY HEAD LIKE A SEED POD!

"SO I'VE GOT TO GET SMALLER STILL. IN FACT...I GET SO SMALL--"
"--I TURN INTO A DREAMBERRY!"
chuckle
dum dee dee dum
BOINK!
"NOW ESCAPE IS EASY. I JUST BOUNCE RIGHT OUT OF A LITTLE HOLE IN THE VAT..."
"...AND ONTO THE FOREST FLOOR!"
DOINK!
"BUT..."
BOINK!
AHH! C'MERE, RIPE 'N' JUICY!
"OH, NO!"
"OH NO!!"
NOOOOO!!

SNORT SNORT
RRRRUUNK!
WOO!! IT'S HIM!!
POP
HUH?!
BOOMPH!
REEEEEEEEEE!
OOOFF!!
...MOTHER...!
SNURT! SNURT!
C'MON! TWIST 'IS NECK!
HELP ME BREAK IT!
OH, RIGHT!

HE'S SPINNING-- EEYAAAH!
pant pant pant
UNNGH! GUH!

pant gasp
DISTRACT 'IM... FINALLY --SOMETHING I CAN USE!
GGGGRRRRRUUUUURRRGH!

LISTEN, PIKE...

...WHEN I SAY "PULL..."

ZHLOOP!
GAAAK!
PULL!!

HUFF! THERE!!
EEYOW!!
CHOKE! KOFF!

RUUUUN!
splutter
HRRUUURGH!
OH, PUCKER-NUTS!

pant pant
ALWAYS A WAY *OUT*, HUH?
ALWAYS! puff pant THAT'S WHAT MY *DREAM* TAUGHT ME.

TAUGHT YOU? A POKING TROLL *ATE* YOU!

I ESCAPED.
HOW?

HOW DO YOU THINK?

sigh OH, DUNG!
THAT'S *EXACTLY* RIGHT, MY CHIEF...

POOT
tee hee hee
"THAT'S EXACTLY RIGHT...!"
DOINK

OOF!
GET OUT OF MY TREE! JUST... GET OUT OF MY TREE!!
REEEEEEEE-UNKH!!
Heh Heh Heh...
pant pant
Whurf!
Heh Heh Heh Heh...
LOSE SOMETHING, LIFEMATE?
YIPE!
SSHOKK!
KRIM... SKOT... NICE KILL!
THANKS!
AND...
WELL, PIKE. YOU SAY ALL OUR DREAMS MEAN SOME-THING...
...AND SOMEDAY YOU'RE GOING TO FIGURE OUT HOW THEY ALL FIT TOGETHER.
I SAY YOU'VE PROVED JUST ONE THING...
YOU CAN ONLY DREAM ABOUT WHAT YOUR HEAD'S STUFFED FULL OF!

PIKE'S RECENT TUSK-HOG KILL IS DIVIDED AMONG THE TRIBE AND WOLF PACK. THE MEAT IS WARM AND RED.
BEFORE THE NIGHT IS DONE, EVERY PART OF THE KILL WILL HAVE BEEN EATEN OR SET ASIDE FOR OTHER USES.
UUMMM! LET'S CELEBRATE OUR AWAKENING WITH THE SMELL OF SMOKE AND THE SIZZLE OF FAT!
I LIKE MY MEAT CHARRED, NOT STILL BREATHING!

NO USE TREADING THAT OLD PATH AGAIN, KRIM.
NO FIRE!
WE'VE BARELY STARTED SCOUTING OUR TERRITORY.
THERE'S NO TELLING HOW STRONG THE "TALL ONES" HAVE GROWN WHILE WE SLEPT.

AND REDLANCE HASN'T BEGUN TO RESHAPE OUR THORN WALL.
NOTHING WE DO MUST GIVE OUR PRESENCE AWAY TO THE HUMANS!

YOU NEVER DID KNOW HOW TO SAY "POKE IT" AND THROW A REAL FEAST, CUTTER!
WOLFRIDERS HAVE NO GIFT FOR MERRY-MAKING --NOT LIKE US GO-BACKS!

HMPH!
HERE WE GO AGAIN!
HIDING OUR TAILS AND WATCHING FOR HUMANS UNDER EVERY ROCK!
AS LONG AS YOU'VE BRED YOUR SHARE OF YOUNG, WHAT'S SO THUMPING IMPORTANT ABOUT KEEPING ALIVE?

YOU AND *I* SEE IT THAT WAY, *SKOT*. CUTTER NEVER WILL. GET USED TO IT.

BESIDES, WE *HAVEN'T* BRED OUR SHARE YET! NO POINT IN SEEKING A WARRIOR'S DEATH 'TIL -- HEY!

THERE!

HALFWAY DOWN THE MOUNTAIN--

"--*SMOKE!*"

"A CAMPFIRE!"

ROAST DEER MEAT... slurp

sn-i-i-ifff

AAAAHHH...!

SOON...
BU-U-U-RRUPP!
HI, PETAL-WING!
WHAT A FEED MY LIFEMATES MISSED! THERE'S NOTHING LEFT!

yawn
THINK I'LL GO TEASE 'EM ABOUT IT.
I'D NEVER GO BELLY-EMPTY JUST TO KICK AGAINST THE RULES!

GUESS THEY'RE STILL SULKING IN OUR TREE-DEN ...
sniff sniff
HUH?! NO SCENTS... NO SOUNDS... NO SKOT AND KRIM!
NOW, WHERE IN...?

APPREHENSIVE, PIKE TRACKS HIS LIFEMATES PARTWAY DOWN THE MOUNTAIN, WHERE...
UH OH! SMOKE...FROM SOME HUMAN'S COOK-FIRE!
SKOT... KRIM... TELL ME YOU'RE NOT THAT WITLESS!

OF COURSE YOU ARE! I KNOW YOU!
YOU WANT IT, YOU GO GET IT--
--AND DUNGBALLS IN THE FACE OF ANY NO-SAYER!
WELL, I WON'T TELL ON YOU...

"I JUST HOPE I DON'T HAVE TO SAVE YOUR STUBBORN NECKS!"
<BE MORE FAITHFUL WITH YOUR TURNING, DUNYONK.>
<LOOK THERE! YOU'VE GONE AND BLACKED OUR SUPPER ON ONE SIDE!>
<Heh Heh Heh... AND WOULD YOU WED ME, WERE I TO MAKE A BETTER JOB OF IT?>
<C'MON! GIVE US A KISS!>
smack smack
BWAAH HAH HAH!
WHO NEEDS TO? THEY DON'T LOOK HALF AS TOUGH AS I REMEMBER.
CAN'T UNDERSTAND A WORD OF THEIR CHATTER.
POKE THAT! JUST MAKE 'EM RUN!
snicker WE'LL MAKE 'EM MESS THEIR BREECHES.

AAAYOOOOAHH!!
HUUUAAAAAAH!!
Gasp
FLY, ROUND-EARS!!
FLY OR DIE!!
SKOT DIVES FOR THE NEAREST WOODSMAN, EXPECTING THE HUMAN TO FIGHT...

...NOT TO COLLAPSE IN ASTONISHMENT!
KRUMPF!
THE FLAMES!!!
CRACKLE!
AAAAGH!!
⟨POOR LAD!⟩
⟨HIS TUNIC'S ABLAZE!⟩
UNH!
AAAGH!
HUNH!
THEY'RE CLOSING IN FOR THE KILL!

NOOOOOO!!
AAAYOOOOOOOAAH!!!
SKOT! KRIM!
< THREKSH'T ABOVE! WHAT'S HAPPENING?! >
< SPIRITS! >
< FOREST SPIRITS! WE'VE ANGERED THEM! >
< THEY'RE AFTER US! RUN!! >
PAT
PAT
PAT
PAT
OH! OOW!
FIRE'S OUT. STRIP 'IM.
Uuuunhh...
gasp HIGH ONES...!
MOMENTS LATER...
C'MON, GNAWBONE, GIMME THAT HAUNCH!
RRR-RRR-RRRH!
WE NEED THE FAT TO DRESS SKOT'S BURNS!

SOON...
KRIM!
GO ON AHEAD! TELL LEETAH TO BE READY!
RIGHT! DON'T BE LONG!

YOU'RE... YOU'RE NOT ANGRY...?
WHY?
THOSE BURNS ARE NOTHING TO THE ROASTING CUTTER'LL GIVE YOU!

I KNOW...
NNGH!

hsss

EASY...

BETWEEN YOU AND ME-- hss --IF I HAD TO CHOOSE A WAY TO GO--
--I'D PICK FIRE LAST!

"DON'T THINK OF THE PAIN, SKOT. I KNOW...! TELL ME A DREAM!"

DREAM?! YOU AND YOUR GAME!
"DOES A WOLF WHO RUNS IN HIS SLEEP REMEMBER WHAT IT WAS HE THOUGHT HE WAS CHASING?"
"GO-BACKS DON'T REMEMBER SLEEP-PICTURES. JUST BEING ALIVE IS LIKE WALKING THROUGH A SNOW-DREAM ANYWAY."
"WHAT'S BEHIND VANISHES IN WHITE. WHAT'S AHEAD IS COVERED IN WHITE."
"ALL YOU CAN SEE IS YOUR FEET, MOVING ONE IN FRONT OF THE OTHER. THAT'S ALL THAT MATTERS."

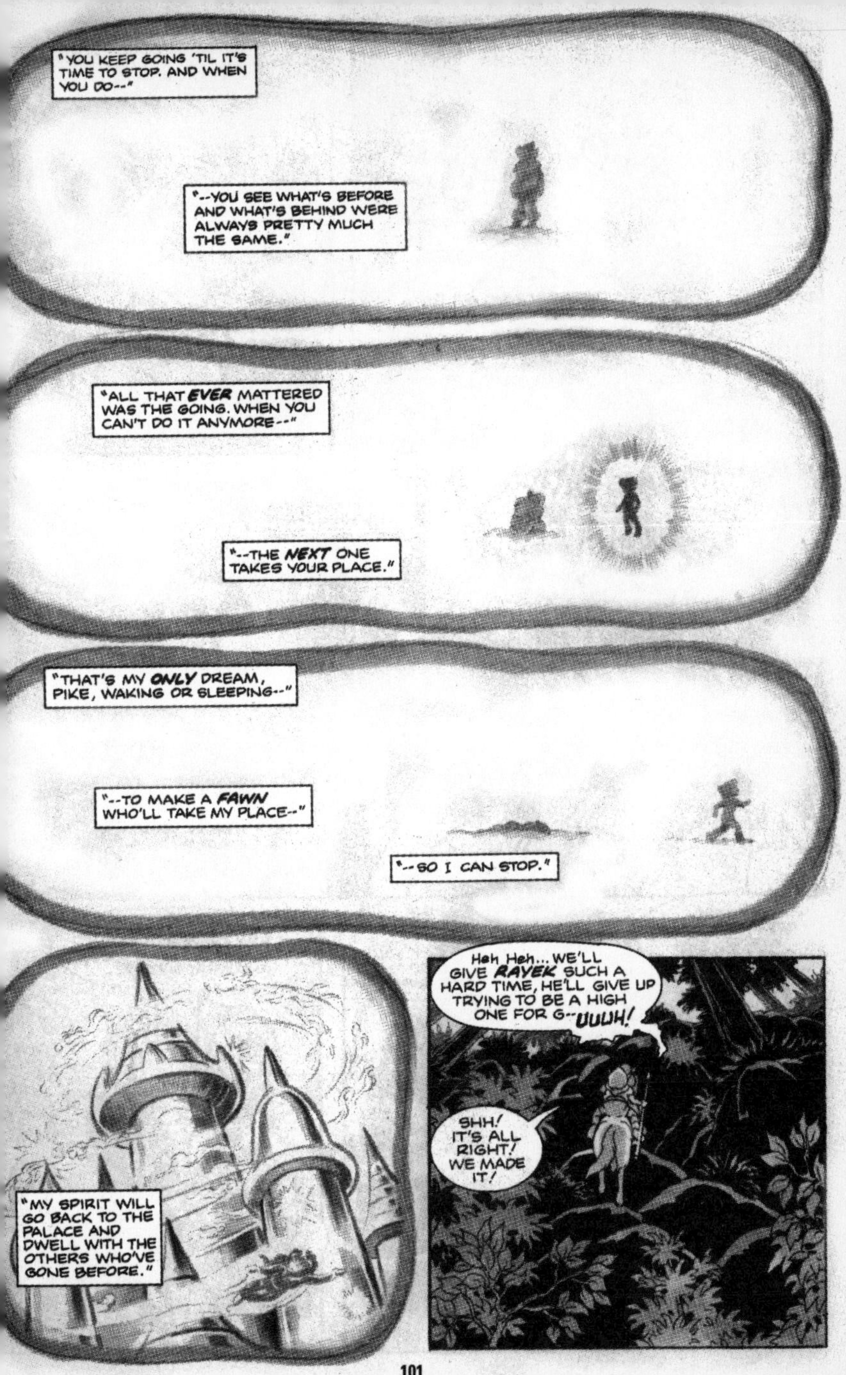
"YOU KEEP GOING 'TIL IT'S TIME TO STOP. AND WHEN YOU DO--"
"--YOU SEE WHAT'S BEFORE AND WHAT'S BEHIND WERE ALWAYS PRETTY MUCH THE SAME."
"ALL THAT EVER MATTERED WAS THE GOING. WHEN YOU CAN'T DO IT ANYMORE--"
"--THE NEXT ONE TAKES YOUR PLACE."
"THAT'S MY ONLY DREAM, PIKE, WAKING OR SLEEPING--"
"--TO MAKE A FAWN WHO'LL TAKE MY PLACE--"
"--SO I CAN STOP."
"MY SPIRIT WILL GO BACK TO THE PALACE AND DWELL WITH THE OTHERS WHO'VE GONE BEFORE."
Heh Heh... WE'LL GIVE RAYEK SUCH A HARD TIME, HE'LL GIVE UP TRYING TO BE A HIGH ONE FOR G--UUUH!
SHH! IT'S ALL RIGHT! WE MADE IT!

AND...
¦sigh¦ HEALER, I ALWAYS SAID YOUR HANDS WERE AS SOOTHING AS WARM--
--MIL-KK!!
SMACK!
YOU FOOL! AFTER SLEEPING THE HIGH ONES KNOW HOW MANY YEARS--
--YOU'D THROW YOUR LIFE AWAY ON A COOKED LEG OF DEER!!
YOU WERE SEEN BY HUMANS! WORSE, YOU ATTACKED THEM!
IF THE OLD HATES ENDED WHILE WE SLEPT, YOU'VE STIRRED THEM UP AGAIN!
GIVE ME ONE GOOD REASON NOT TO DRIVE YOU BOTH OUT-- FOREVER!
PLEASE, CUTTER! WE WOLFRIDERS LEARNED TO CARE ABOUT WHAT'S BEEN AND WHAT'S TO BE.
BUT SKOT AND KRIM NEVER DID.

THINK OF THE DREAMS YOU'VE HEARD SO FAR-- SO MANY FEARS FROM YESTERDAY-- AND FEARS FOR TOMORROW.
SOME OF US FIGHT THEM...
SOME OF US FALL TO THEM...
SOME OF US FLEE FROM THEM...
AND SOME OF US FLY ABOVE THEM!
FEARS MAKE US WANT TO PROTECT WHAT WE HAVE ... SO WE CAN KEEP GOING.
BUT SKOT AND KRIM LIVE A PART OF THE WAY WE'VE LOST SIGHT OF.
THEY TRULY LIVE IN THE "NOW OF WOLF THOUGHT."
CUTTER... DON'T BLAME THEM FOR THAT.
grrr...
VERY WELL.

ALL THE SAME...
MOON-SHADE AND I WILL TAKE THESE TWO IN HAND!
THE WAY HAS OTHER WISDOM THEY NEED REMINDING OF!
OWTCH!

NICE SHOT, LEETAH!
.....

SHOW SOME RESPECT!
I WAS!
I LIKE IT WHEN OUR CHIEF AND HEALER BEAR THEIR FANGS!

THEN YOU'RE GOING TO LOVE DEALING WITH ME!

IN A SHALLOW STONE PIT FORMED BY EKUAR THE ROCK-SHAPER, TWO DEERSKINS CURE IN A REEKING SOLUTION OF TREE BARK, LEGLIFT WATER AND BRINE.
GRUDGINGLY, UNDER THE CRITICAL GAZE OF TRIBAL TANNER MOONSHADE, GO-BACK MAIDEN KRIM DOES PENANCE FOR LAST NIGHT'S DELIBERATE MISBEHAVIOR.
...THEN, AFTER TWO FULL CHANGES OF MOTHER MOON, WE'LL TAKE THE HIDES OUT, POUND AND STRETCH THEM.
PHEW!
I'D RATHER BE SNIFFING MOONS-OLD FISH GUTS!
SCRAPE SCRAPE SCRAPE
THIS IS AS FAR FROM MY FAVORITE PASTIME AS YOU COULD GET ME!
DREAMTIME
THAT'S THE IDEA. KEEP SCRAPING!

SHOW BY YOUR DEEDS THAT YOU'RE TRULY SORRY FOR REVEALING YOURSELF TO THE HUMANS--
--AND CUTTER JUST MIGHT FORGIVE YOU.
WILL YOU...?
WE'LL SEE.

Heh Heh Heh...
...THAT FLOWERLIKE FACE NEVER FOOLED ME, MOONSHADE!
HARD AS BRIGHTMETAL, AREN'T YOU?
NOT SO HARD AS STRONGBOW!

"YOU CAN THANK THE HIGH ONES YOU'RE NOT IN SKOT'S BOOTS RIGHT NOW!"
THERE! YOU'VE SEEN IT MANY TIMES.
GRRRRRR!
GROWRR!
THE CHIEF WOLF PUTS DOWN REBELLION WITHIN THE PACK.
OW! CUT IT OUT!

I TOLD YOU! NO TALKING! SEND!
BAP!
NOW, IF THE LOW-RANKING WOLF IS TOO STUBBORN TO SUBMIT--

GRURRR-RRR!
YIII YIII YIII
"--THE ONES HIGHER UP WILL LEAVE HIM BLOODY... OR WORSE!"
SNARRRGLE!

LEARN FROM THIS!
GO TO CUTTER. SHOW HIM THROAT.
wimper whine
lap lap lap

IF YOU DON'T, AT YOUR SLIGHTEST NEXT SLIP, HE'LL CAST YOU OUT!
AND NONE OF US WILL DEFEND YOU!

UNDER-STOOD...?
URGH! I HATE TRYING TO SEND! IT MAKES MY HEAD ACHE!
IF YOU PRACTICED MORE AND TALKED LESS, YOU'D FEEL AS ONE WITH THE TRIBE.

YOU'D NEVER REPEAT THE SELFISH ERRORS THAT CAUSE US ALL TROUBLE.
DUTY, DUTY, DUTY!
C'MON, ARROW-HEAD! YOU KNOW YOU LOVE ME!
sigh...

OF COURSE YOU'RE LOVED! BUT YOU COULD BE BETTER RESPECTED ...
...IF YOU TRULY WANTED TO.

SHORTLY...
WELL, LIFEMATE, GET YOUR TAIL TUCKED UNDER FOR YOU?
......

WYL...?
...I FEAR THESE GO-BACKS WILL NEVER TAKE "THE WAY" SERIOUSLY!

HMPH! ALWAYS LOCK-SENDING ...FULL OF SECRETS!
BECAUSE WE CAN'T TRUST YOU TO PUT THE TRIBE'S GOOD FIRST!
UH OH!

THAT DOES IT!
YOU HIDE-BOUND ELDERS THINK YOU'RE BETTER THAN US!
THINK YOU'RE HIGH ONES!
WHOA, SKOT! THEY MIGHT AS WELL BE!

SO WHAT?! GO-BACKS TREAT EVERYONE THE SAME!
HE MEANS WE DON'T GROW OLD, IF WE CAN HELP IT--
--SO WE DON'T LEARN TO RESPECT AGE!

AT LEAST WE CAN LAUGH WITH TREESTUMP AND CLEAR-BROOK!
BUT A FERN LAUGHS MORE THAN STRONG-BOW!
AND NEITHER OF YOU SHARE!
THERE'S NO GETTING CLOSE TO YOU!
IS THAT WHAT YOU THINK?

SIT!
???

OOOHH...!
NNNH...!

T-TOO STRONG!
IT HURTS!
WE KNOW

BUT *THIS* IS WHAT YOU WANT.
WORDS AREN'T ENOUGH.
BODIES AREN'T ENOUGH.
THIS IS HOW *WE* SHARE.

"YOU DECIDE HOW CLOSE IS TOO CLOSE."
"YOU SET THE BOUNDARIES...WE WILL HONOR THEM."
"HERE WE ARE ONE, AND AGE MEANS NOTHING."
"COME. ENTER OUR DREAM."

...THAT OUR HEADS, OUR HEARTS, OUR RULES WERE SMALL --

--AND THAT STANDING OVER YOU MADE US FEEL BIG?

WE...OUR WOLF-FRIENDS... WE'RE ALL JUST BITS OF FLESH, SWIRLING IN A VASTDEEP SEA WHERE ALL IS POSSIBLE!

NOTHING EVER GETS DONE -NOTHING CAN- UNLESS WE ABIDE BY THE RULES WE MAKE.

AND SO...

Hmmm...WHAT D'YOU THINK I'LL HAVE TO TRADE OLD *PICKNOSE* FOR A TWO-BLADED AXE, EH, *CUTTER*?

DUNNO, *TREESTUMP*. BETTER CATCH 'IM WHILE HE'S STILL SOFT AS NUT-MASH FROM GETTING TRINKET BACK.

GO ON, SILLY-- HE WON'T *BITE* YOU!

DON'T BE SO SURE, *SHEN-SHEN*!

HSSHT! SHUT UP, WILL YOU?

Heh
Heh
Heh...
...ALL RIGHT!
TAIL IT OUT OF HERE BEFORE I NIP YOUR GRINNING MUZZLE OFF!

NOW, WHY DON'T I EVER TRY THAT ON CUTTER?
YEEEHOOoo!!
OH, PIKE! COME OUT OF YOUR DREAMBERRY FOG!
SKOT PICKED THAT TRICK UP FROM YOU!

TYLEET! SHENSHEN!
MY RUMP IS SAVED!!
giggle
WONDERFUL! NOW, CAN YOU KEEP IT OUT OF TROUBLE?

THAT DEPENDS! UP FOR A LITTLE PLAY, LOVELY MAIDENS?
NOTHING SOUL-PIERCING! NOTHING DEEP! NO SKULL-ACHES!
WOOOOO! NO ARGUMENTS FROM ME!
chuckle

CUTTER HAS FORGIVEN, BUT THE TALL ONES WON'T FORGET.
THEY CAPTURED LEETAH DAYS AGO.
AND OTHERS SAW SKOT AND KRIM LAST NIGHT.

THEY KNOW WE'RE HERE.
BEFRIENDING THEM IS OUR BEST HOPE...
...AND MY FONDEST DREAM...

WOLFRIDERS HUNT, HOWL, GUARD AND PLAY. IN THEIR PREDATORY WORLD, NOTHING THEY CREATE IS EXPECTED TO LAST... NOTHING IS MEANT TO.
PIKE'S NOTION OF COLLECTING DREAMS TO FIND THE COMMON THREAD WHICH BINDS THEM IS STILL VERY NEW AND STRANGE TO HIS TRIBE.
PERHAPS I UNDERSTAND YOUR DREAM GAME BEST... BECAUSE I'VE BEEN CLOSER TO A HUMAN THAN ANY OF THE OTHERS.
AND HUMANS ALWAYS TRY TO HANG ON TO THINGS, EH, TYLEET?
HEH HEH! LEAVE IT TO ME TO TRY KEEPING WHAT NO HAND CAN HOLD!
DREAMTIME PT. 6
WHEN IT COMES TO THE TALL ONES, MOST OF US WANT TO LIVE AND LET LIVE.
BUT I HOPE A TIME WILL COME WHEN WE LEARN FROM THEM-- HELP THEM-- AND THEY DO AS MUCH FOR US!

IN MY DREAM, WORDS OPEN THE PATH TO FRIEND-SHIP.
THEY AREN'T ENOUGH. BUT THEY MAKE GOOD BEGINNINGS.
"I ALWAYS WONDERED WHAT MY CUBLING LITTLE PATCH DREAMT OF, FOR WE COULDN'T SEND TO EACH OTHER."
"IN THE SLEEP-VISIO I RECALL BEST, HE WANDERS OUT OF THE WOODS INTO AN OPEN FIELD."
"BEYOND IT LIES A SETTLEMENT BUILT BY MANY HUMANS. IT LOOKS VERY ODD..."
"...TALLER THAN SHENSHEN'S SENDING-PICTURES OF THE SUN VILLAGE'S HUTS."
"I DON'T WANT LITTLE PATCH TO GO THERE."
"TO BE SURE, THAT'S JUST WHAT HE DID WHEN HE WAS GROWN..."
"...BUT IN MY DREAM, MY FEELINGS ARE ALL THOSE OF A SHE-WOLF PROTECTING A TINY CUB."
"I GIVE CHASE. BUT MY LEGS MOVE SO SLOWLY! IT'S AS IF I'M STRUGGLING AGAINST THE CURRENT OF A SWOLLEN STREAM!"

"BEFORE I CAN REACH HIM, LITTLE PATCH HAS TODDLED ACROSS THE FIELD, RIGHT INTO THAT QUEER, BUSY PLACE FULL OF HUMANS."
"I LOSE HIM SO QUICKLY AMONG THE TWO-LEGGED HERD."
"WHERE ARE THEY ALL GOING? WHAT ARE THEY ALL UP TO..."
"...THAT THEY CAN'T STOP A MOMENT TO TEND A MOTHERLESS CUB?"
"NEXT TO PATCH, I'M THE SMALLEST HERE. I SEE NOTHING BUT WIDE-STRIDING LEGS."
"HOW FRIGHTENING IT MUST BE FOR HIM!"
"TO ALL MY CALLS, THERE IS NO ANSWERING CRY."

"THE TALL ONES NOTICE ME IN MY SEARCH, AND STARE. THEY DON'T SEEM TO BE AFRAID."
"I DARE TO ASK FOR HELP. BUT THEY CAN'T UNDERSTAND ME."
"EVEN SO, THEY SENSE MY NEED."
"THE FIRST TO COME FORWARD ARE THE FRIENDLY ONES..."
"...NONNA AND ADAR! FROM WHAT I'VE HEARD, I KNOW THEY'LL HELP FIND LITTLE PATCH."
"BUT, TO MY SURPRISE, THEIR WORDS ARE JUST GABBLE!"
"I LISTEN CLOSELY, UNTIL THEIR MEANING SOMEHOW COMES CLEAR."
"THEN I TRY IMITATING THEIR STRANGE TALK."
"MY MOUTH SHAPES IT POORLY, AT FIRST."
"THEN THE WORDS TAKE FORM...BECOMING LOUDER, MORE SURE..."
"AT LAST I'M ABLE TO SAY..."
I HAVE A HUMAN SON-- LITTLE PATCH.
HE IS LOST AMONG YOU. WILL YOU HELP?

"SADLY, ONCE MY WORDS ARE UNDERSTOOD, MY DEEDS ARE NOT."
"WHEN THEY LEARN I'VE RAISED ONE OF THEIR KIND, SOME OF THEM ARE GREATLY OFFENDED."
"THEY DISTRUST ME AND TURN AWAY BECAUSE..."
"...IN THE END, I'M NOT ONE OF THEM."
"I GO ON ALONE, CALLING IN HUMAN TONGUE."
LITTLE PATCH!
LITTLE PATCH!
COME BACK!
"THE HUMAN HERD IS BIG IN EVERY WAY, AND I AM VERY SMALL."
"THEY'VE SNATCHED MY CUB, I KNOW IT! THEY THINK HE BELONGS WITH THEM!"
NO...
...NOT YET!
NOT YET!
sob sob
"SOMEONE HUGE COMES UP BEHIND."
"AM I NOW TO PAY WITH MY FREEDOM, MERELY FOR ASKING THEIR HELP?"

"NO! IT'S THE GRUFF, KINDLY ONE CUTTER HAS TOLD OF..."
"...THAT GREAT BEAR OF A HUMAN, OLBAR, WHO LIFTS ME HIGH ABOVE THE HERD!"
"NO ONE QUESTIONS, OR EVEN LOOKS SIDEWAYS AS WE PASS."
LITTLE PATCH! LITTLE PATCH!
WHERE ARE YOU, MY SON?!
"I LOOK OVER THE FLOCK OF BOBBING HEADS AND..."
"I SEE I'M TRUSTED AFTER ALL!"
"THEY'VE FOUND HIM! THEY'RE BRINGING HIM TO ME!"
"WHY? WHAT HAS CHANGED?"
"AS I CUDDLE MY PRECIOUS CUB, I SEE THE ANSWER AT ONCE..."

"I *AM* ONE OF THEM! I HAVE *FIVE* FINGERS ON EACH HAND!"

"THROUGH THIS DREAM-GIFT, I'VE LIVED THE NEED LITTLE PATCH MUST HAVE KNOWN ALL HIS LIFE..."

...THE NEED TO BE ACCEPTED.

MAYBE IT'S ONLY IN DREAMS THAT THINGS TURN OUT SO WELL.

WELL, SHENSHEN! DID YOU SHOW *SKOT* ANY NEW *ROMPS*?

OH, I DON'T KNOW...

THERE'S SOMETHING TO BE SAID FOR OLD FAVORITES! giggle

AS FOR THINGS TURNING OUT... IF I COULD MAKE FRIENDS, OF SORTS, WITH THAT GROUCHY *OLD MAGGOTY*...

...*ANYTHING* IS POSSIBLE!

"WELL, I'M BACK IN SORROW'S END. AND, AS USUAL, LEETAH OUTSHINES ME IN EVERY WAY."
"I PLAY THE SIDE-WATCHER CHEERFULLY, AS I ALWAYS DO."
"PART OF ME KNOWS SHE WILL DISAPPEAR SOON. THE SOONER THE BETTER!"
"I'M WICKED! IT'S SHAMEFUL, I KNOW!"
"BUT MY DREAM-SELF DOESN'T CARE HOW MUCH I'LL MISS HER!"
"I HURRY TO SAVAH'S HUT..."
"...AND ASK THE WISE MOTHER OF MEMORY..."
WHAT WILL MAKE ME SHINE BRIGHTER THAN LEETAH... EVEN JUST ONCE?

"SAVAH PROMISES TO SHOW ME SOMETHING."
"IT MAKES ME SO HAPPY! I ALWAYS DEPEND ON HER GUIDANCE!"
"SHE LEADS ME DOWNSTAIRS TO HER PRIVATE, UNDERGROUND CHAMBER."
"BUT, OH MY! THE STAIRS TURN INTO A TUNNEL AND THE ELEGANT CHAMBER BECOMES A DANK, SMELLY CAVE."
"AND SAVAH... ¡giggle! THIS IS SO SILLY!"
"SAVAH TURNS INTO OLD MAGGOTY!"
"SHE GOES GAB-GAB-GABBING AWAY, JUST LIKE SHE ALWAYS DOES."
"I SAY I DON'T QUITE UNDERSTAND..."
"...AND THAT MAKES HER VERY, VERY ANGRY!"
!!**??¿!!!

"SHE MAKES IT CLEAR MY TASK IS TO PICK CERTAIN ROOTS AND MUSHROOMS AND PLACE THEM IN HER BASKET."
"I GRUDGINGLY OBEY..."
"...THOUGH IT'S PAST ME HOW THIS WILL HELP ME SHINE APART FROM MY SISTER!"
"MY TROLL TEACHER CERTAINLY HAS SOME LESSON IN MIND, FOR EACH TIME I REACH TO PLUCK UP A TREASURE--"
"A GREAT BOOT STOMPS DOWN AND CRUSHES IT!"
"IT HAPPENS AGAIN--"
"--AND AGAIN!"

"AND THEN...IT ALMOST HAPPENS TO ME!"
"BUT I 'WAKE UP' JUST IN TIME!"
{cackle cackle} A DREAM WITHIN A DREAM!
"HMPH! WITH WHATEVER OLD MAGGOTY THINKS IS FUNNY, I SELDOM AGREE."
"THERE IS A THUNDEROUS RUMBLING ABOVE. THE CAVE WALLS SHUDDER AND START TO SQUEEZE IN!"
AM-- AM I DREAMING...? RIGHT NOW?
Hee Hee Heee! LITTLE DUNCE! DREAMS NEVER HAPPEN "NOW!"
"NOW I'M THE ANGRY ONE!"
NO MORE TRICKS! TELL ME HOW TO OUTSHINE LEETAH!
YOU'LL COME INTO YOUR OWN, PIGLET PIE!

" 'BUT NOT WHEN YOU THINK YOU OUGHT,' SHE SAYS."
THEN WHEN?
WHEN?
"OLD MAGGOTY JUST LAUGHS. THE CAVE IS DARK, STIFLING, CLOSING IN!"
"CAN'T BREATHE! I MUST FLEE OR CHOKE!"
"BUT THERE, ON THE GROUND BEFORE ME, LIES MY BEAUTIFUL SISTER! I CAN'T LEAVE HER!"
OH, LEETAH! I'M DREAMING IN A DARK CAVE, BECAUSE OF YOU!
WHEN WILL I SEE MY OWN LIGHT?!
"NOW THIS YOU'LL LIKE! LEETAH TURNS OVER AND..."
"...SHE'S YOU, TYLEET! AND YOU SAY..."
SHINE-- WHERE YOU LOVE!
"THEN YOU SHOW ME YOU ARE WITH CUB! YOU HOLD OUT YOUR HAND AND..."
"...IT HAS FIVE FINGERS!"

AND...?
AND THAT'S ALL. THAT'S WHEN THE TROLLS SLICED OPEN MY COCOON!
MY FIVE FINGERS... IN *YOUR* DREAM TOO.
WE *MUST* HAVE TOUCHED THOUGHTS AS WE SLEPT!
OH, I HOPE YOUR VISION OF ME WITH CUB COMES TRUE!
TO ME IT FEELS AS IF IT ALREADY HAS!
OH, *PUCKER-NUTS!*
GET IT!
THANK-YOUTHANK-YOUTHANK-YOU!
WHOOSH!
??!
CUTTER! I FOUND IT!
I FOUND THE *THREAD!*
YOU HAVE TO CALL COUNCIL *NOW!*
HUH?
WHAT'S UP, PIKE?
THE DREAM GAME! IT'S ALMOST DONE, CUTTER! I'LL EXPLAIN--
--SOON AS YOU, *AROREE* AND *CLEARBROOK* HAVE TOLD YOURS!
BEFORE THE ENTIRE TRIBE?! *BAT DUNG!*

"LET'S GET IT OVER WITH!"

SILENTLY, ONE BY ONE, CUTTER STUDIES EACH FACE IN THE COUNCIL OF WOLFRIDERS.
HIS EYES LINGER LONGEST ON THE FEATURES OF HIS LIFEMATE, CHILDREN AND BROTHER... THE FAMILY SO LONG LOST TO HIM AND, INCREDIBLY, HIS ONCE MORE.
IT WAS NOT CUTTER'S WISH TO CALL THE TRIBE TOGETHER THIS NIGHT. SAVE FOR THE PROMPTINGS OF TIMMAIN, THE HIGH ONE IN WOLF GUISE, HE WOULD NOT HAVE DONE SO.
NOT, AT LEAST, FOR THE REASON PIKE NOW VOICES.
FOR DAYS, NOW, I'VE BEEN GATHERING YOUR DREAMS LIKE SEEDS...
DREAMTIME
PART 10
...AND IT HASN'T BEEN THE SIMPLEST TASK, I CAN TELL YOU!

SOME OF YOU "PODS" HAVE BEEN HARDER TO PRY OPEN THAN OTHERS!
gr-r-r-umble
AND SOME "POD PAIRS" HAVE SHARED BUT ONE SEED BETWEEN THEM!
SKOT SPOKE FOR ME, LIFEMATE, THAT'S SURE!

MY DREAMS HAVE ALWAYS BEEN SIMPLE, PIKE. UNTIL NOW, I'VE NEVER GIVEN THEM MUCH THOUGHT.
IN THEM I RELIVE HUNTS AND HOWLS...
...AND SMALL PLEASURES WITH MY LIFEMATE -- THE STUFF OF EVERY DAY.
IT WAS NO DIFFERENT DURING THE LONG SLEEP. EXCEPT...
EXCEPT...?
I RECALL HAVING ONE DREAM WHEREIN I KNEW I DREAMED...
...AND WISHED WITH ALL MY BEING THAT I COULD WAKE!
"IT TOOK ME BACK TO THE DAYS JUST AFTER THE FIRST WAR FOR THE PALACE. DAYS THAT HELD SOME PEACE..."
"...BUT MORE OFTEN CONFUSION, AS WE TRIED TO REMAKE OUR LIVES IN THE FORBIDDEN GROVE."
"WITH OUR FINDING OF THE PALACE, OUR KNOWING OF THE WORLD AND OUR PLACE IN IT WAS ALL UNSETTLED."
"AGAINST THE WAY, WE LIVED IN FEAR... FEAR OF SENDING... FEAR OF HAVING OUR VERY SOULS SNATCHED BY THE BLACK SNAKE."
"DOES ANYONE REMEMBER?"

I DO. AFTER THE WAR IT SEEMED, FOR A TIME, THE WAY WENT DIM BEFORE ME.
THE MORE I TRIED TO THINK AND PLAN US ALL OUT OF TROUBLE, THE MORE TANGLED EVERYTHING GOT.
IN THE END, GUESSES AND LUCK WERE ALL I COULD COUNT ON.
AYE. IT WASN'T THE CLEAREST OF TIMES FOR ANY OF US.
DREAMS AREN'T ALWAYS KIND. SOMETIMES THEY MAKE US RELIVE MOMENTS WE'D JUST AS SOON FORGET.
OR MAKE US SEE THINGS WE HOPE WE'LL NEVER LIVE TO SEE!
"BLUE MOUNTAIN WAS A TWISTED, UNNATURAL PLACE, TO BE SURE. BUT IN MY DREAM, IT'S EVEN MORE SO."
"I'M DEEP INSIDE, SEARCHING FOR WINDKIN."
"THE KIDNAPPED CUB IS HELD CAPTIVE SOMEWHERE IN THIS DISEASED STRONGHOLD."

"THOUGH I'VE BEEN HERE BEFORE, I DON'T KNOW MY WAY ABOUT. THERE IS NO SCENT TRAIL TO FOLLOW."
"IT MADDENS ME THAT I DARE NOT SEND TO THE CUB, BECAUSE THE BLACK SNAKE MIGHT CATCH MY THOUGHTS... AND ME."
"I TRAVEL THROUGH NARROW PASSAGEWAYS, LOST AND FULL OF FEAR."
"MY HEART POUNDS IN MY THROAT. I PANT HARD, UNABLE TO CATCH MY BREATH."
"THE STONE WALLS ARE DARK AND COVERED WITH RAISED SYMBOLS."
"THEY COME TO LIFE AND THREATEN!"
"BUT I MOVE PAST THEM AND CONTINUE THE SEARCH FOR THE CUB."

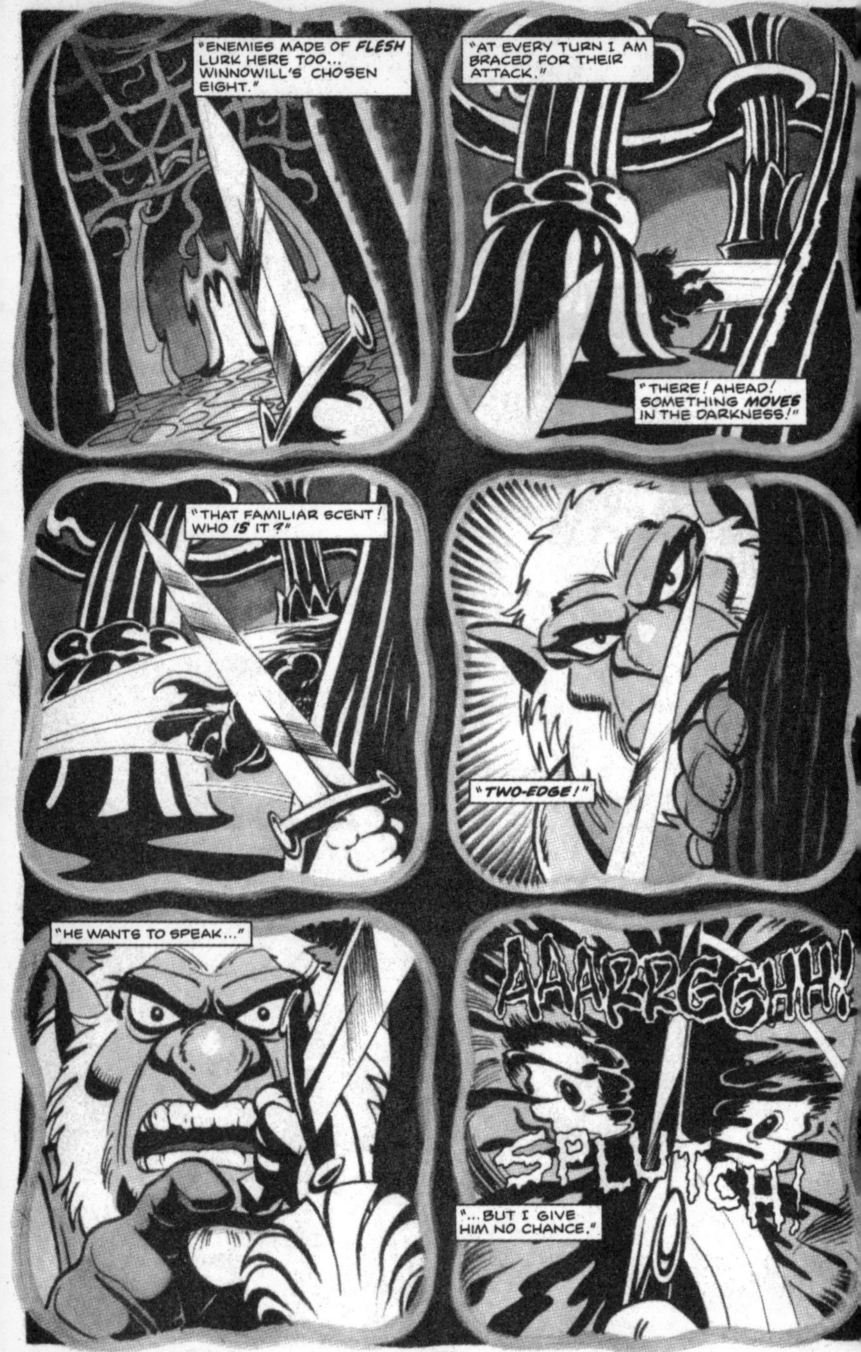
"ENEMIES MADE OF FLESH LURK HERE TOO... WINNOWILL'S CHOSEN EIGHT."
"AT EVERY TURN I AM BRACED FOR THEIR ATTACK."
"THERE! AHEAD! SOMETHING MOVES IN THE DARKNESS!"
"THAT FAMILIAR SCENT! WHO IS IT?"
"TWO-EDGE!"
"HE WANTS TO SPEAK..."
AAARRGGHH!
SPLUTCH!
"...BUT I GIVE HIM NO CHANCE."

"AFIRE WITH RAGE AND FEAR COMBINED, I PLUNGE ONWARD."
"THE LITTLE CUB'S HOWLING! IT GUIDES ME!"
"AROUND THE NEXT BEND..."
"...I COME UPON THE BLACK SNAKE HERSELF!"
Heh Heh Heh Heh Heh
WAAAH! AAWAAAA!
"SHE CLUTCHES WINDKIN IN HER COILS! I KNOW WHAT HER POISON CAN DO TO ME..."
"...TO HIM
"BUT MY DREAM-SELF HAS NO WISDOM."
"THE FURY BLAZING WITHIN MY HEART CAN BE QUENCHED ONLY BY HER BLOOD!"
"gasp! AGAIN, TWO-EDGE!"
"AGAIN HE WOULD HAVE WORDS!"
"AGAIN I CUT HIM DOWN BEFORE HE CAN UTTER THEM!"
GAAAAH!
FWAASHH!

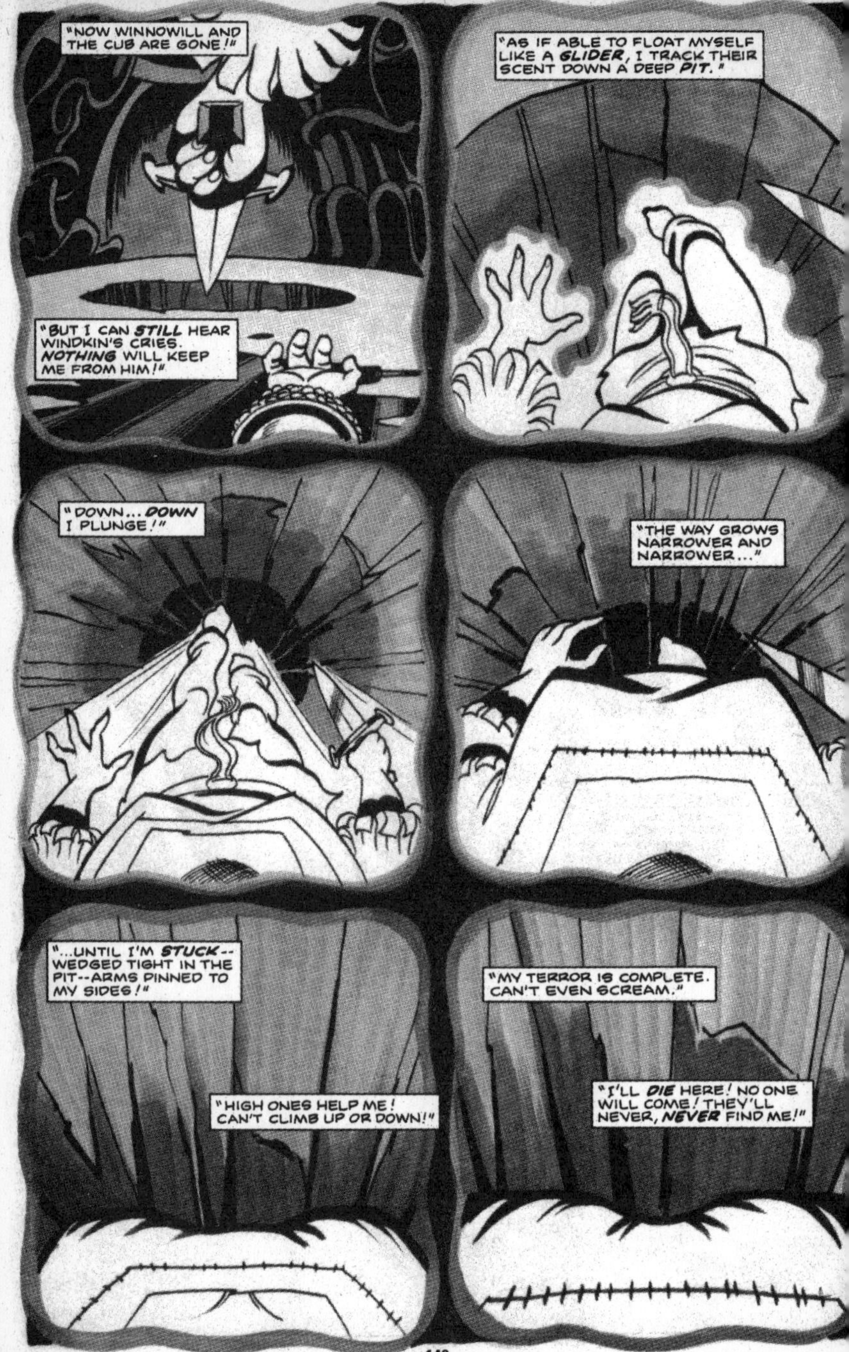
"NOW WINNOWILL AND THE CUB ARE GONE!"
"BUT I CAN STILL HEAR WINDKIN'S CRIES. NOTHING WILL KEEP ME FROM HIM!"
"AS IF ABLE TO FLOAT MYSELF LIKE A GLIDER, I TRACK THEIR SCENT DOWN A DEEP PIT."
"DOWN... DOWN I PLUNGE!"
"THE WAY GROWS NARROWER AND NARROWER..."
"...UNTIL I'M STUCK-- WEDGED TIGHT IN THE PIT--ARMS PINNED TO MY SIDES!"
"HIGH ONES HELP ME! CAN'T CLIMB UP OR DOWN!"
"MY TERROR IS COMPLETE. CAN'T EVEN SCREAM."
"I'LL DIE HERE! NO ONE WILL COME! THEY'LL NEVER, NEVER FIND ME!"

"AND THEN..."
RAP! RAP!
KRAK KRAK-KRAK!
"...THE WALL BEFORE ME SHATTERS."
K-K-KRUMMBLE!
"TWO-EDGE, ALIVE AND WHOLE DESPITE MY BEST THRUSTS, WORKS TO RELEASE ME!"
"'BUT-BUT I KILLED YOU,' I SAY."
NO. YOU DIDN'T.
"IT'S TRUE! NOW I KNOW THAT I AM DREAMING!"
"'THEN WINDKIN IS ALREADY SAFE,' I SAY."
NO. HE IS NOT.
CHILDREN ARE NEVER SAFE.
NONE OF US EVER ARE...
NONE OF US...
NONE OF US...
NONE OF US...

THAT'S ALL.
WHOOF! LIKE-- BUT NOT LIKE --WHAT REALLY HAPPENED!
TWO-EDGE DID SAVE YOU AND WINDKIN!

BUT MY TRUE ACTIONS, THANK THE HIGH ONES, WEREN'T SO RASH AS THOSE OF MY DREAM-SELF.
I HOPE I WENT ON TO SOME OTHER, CALMER VISION.

YOU DID!
AROREE! YOU SHARED A DREAM WITH CLEARBROOK?

SHARED?
NO...
...VISITED!
IF EVER I HAD A DREAM OF MY OWN...

...IT HAPPENED TOO LONG AGO FOR ME TO RECALL, MUCH LESS TELL OF IT!
LOVE-MATE...?

WHY DO YOU SEEM SO... ASHAMED?
YOUR TRIBE TOOK ME IN, SKYWISE...
...TRUSTED ME AS ONE OF THEM. NOW THEY MUST LEARN WHAT I DID AS I SLEPT THE LONG SLEEP...
...THOUGH IT COSTS ME THAT TRUST FOREVER!

IT FROZE MY BLOOD TO LEARN, UPON WAKING, THAT LORD WINNOWILL STILL LIVES.
SHE IS NOT THE ONLY ONE WHO FEEDS ON DREAMS.
"SHE TAUGHT THAT TRICK TO HER CHOSEN EIGHT AS WELL..."
"...TAUGHT US TO VISIT OTHERS' SLEEPING MINDS IN SUBTLE, SECRET WAYS...UNDETECTABLE!"
"BUT THE COST WAS HIGH--TERRIBLY HIGH!"
"IN TIME, WE LOST THE ABILITY TO DREAM FOR OURSELVES."
"THE EMPTINESS--UNBEARABLE! IT SET US ALL A FEATHER'S BREADTH AWAY FROM MADNESS!"

MY LITTLE LOVE, YOU CANNOT KNOW WHAT IT IS TO LAY YOUR HEAD DOWN...
...AND SLIP INTO A NOTHINGNESS BLACKER THAN DEATH!

TO BE AWARE THAT, BECAUSE YOU ARE NOT DEAD, YOU SHOULD BE DREAMING... BUT CAN'T!
IT'S WRONG TO ENTER OTHERS' THOUGHTS UNASKED.

THAT'S WHY, IN OUR BRIEF TIME TOGETHER, YOU NEVER SAW ME SLEEP.
AND IN ALL YOUR SEASONS HERE ON THORNY MOUNTAIN, YOU NEVER SLEPT EITHER?!

HIGH ONES! HOW BRAVE YOU WERE TO LET YOURSELF BE COCOONED WITH THE REST!
!!!
BRAVE INDEED... CONSIDERING!

DEAR TRIBEMATES! YOU DON'T ABHOR MY SECRET VISITATIONS, THEN?
THEY WERE ONLY FOR COMFORT, AROREE.
HOLD IT!

YOU MEAN I'VE SPENT DAYS **WHEEDLING** SLEEP VISIONS--
--OUT OF THE **SURLIEST** OF THIS BUNCH, WHILE ALL THE TIME **YOU**--?!

OH, PIKE! EVERY DREAM THAT'S BEEN TOLD SINCE YOUR GAME BEGAN...
...I HAVE KNOWN IN **DETAIL** ALREADY!

AND **MORE** BESIDES.

THEN... **YOU** UNDERSTAND.

ALL TOO WELL, MY CHIEF.

HMPH! AND I THOUGHT **I'D** IMPRESS EVERYONE BY UNTYING MY BAG OF DREAM-SEEDS TONIGHT!
BUT IT'S **AROREE** AND **CUTTER** WHO'VE HELD THE COMMON THREAD ALL ALONG!
MAKE NO MISTAKE. YOUR DREAM-GAME **HAS** SERVED A GOOD PURPOSE, PIKE.

IT'S MADE US A CLOSE-KNIT PACK AGAIN...
HELPED US EACH TO RELEARN OUR PLACE AND OUR DUTIES.
BUT MY ADVICE AS CHIEF IS...
...LET THE GAME END *NOW*!
OUR ONLY TASK, IN THIS NEW TIME, IS TO BE WHAT WE ARE... *WOLFRIDERS*!
TO LIVE *THE WAY*, NO MATTER HOW MUCH THE FOREST, THE LAND AND EVEN THE *ENTIRE WORLD* HAVE CHANGED!

CUT THE THREAD, PIKE! SCATTER YOUR DREAM-SEEDS AND LET THEM GROW WILD!
THEY'LL BEAR BLOSSOMS OR THORNS IN THEIR *OWN* TIME. DON'T RUSH THINGS.
CUTTER...

"WHAT'S *YOUR* DREAM?"
......

UUH... UM, *HEY*!
SNAP!
DON'T *I* GET A TURN?

ALL THE DREAMS HAVE NOW BEEN TOLD, ONE APIECE, BY THOSE WHO SLEPT THE LONG SLEEP IN THE NEW LAND...
...ALL, THAT IS, SAVE CUTTER'S. TO HIS GREAT RELIEF, HIS MOMENT MUST WAIT AS...
BUT--BUT YOU WEREN'T COCOONED WITH THE REST OF US, SKYWISE!
SO? YOU WON'T KNOW IF MY DREAM FITS IN OR NOT 'TIL YOU HEAR IT!
HE'S RIGHT! REMEMBER, IN MY SLEEP-VISION OLD MAGGOTY SAID DREAMS NEVER HAPPEN "NOW."
DREAMTIME
Pt. 11
SEEMS TO ME THEY'RE ALL FOR FUN, SHENSHEN... A WAY FOR OUR SPIRITS TO PLAY WHILE OUR BODIES REST!

OH YOU DO, DO YOU?
Hmph! YOU THINK MY DREAM... OR NIGHTFALL'S... WAS "FUN," CUB?
SCARY FUN, TREE-STUMP...
...BECAUSE THEY NEVER HAPPENED, ANY MORE THAN THE ONE I HAD YESTERDAY DID!
I ONLY WISH IT COULD! LISTEN...
"IT'S NIGHT. I'M ALL ALONE ON A HILLTOP, GUARDING A CART. DUNNO WHY."
"IT'S FULL OF TREASURE -- PIECES OF GOLD! -- ALL TIED IN NEAT BUNDLES AND STACKED IN A BIG PILE."
"THERE'S AN EXTRA BAG I KNOW IS MINE!"
"HEH HEH... I MAKE SURE IT DOESN'T GET MIXED IN WITH THE BIG TREASURE!"

"SUDDENLY I HEAR HOOFBEATS! HUMANS... RIDING NOHUMPS!"
"THEY'RE SEARCHING FOR THE CART, THE TREASURE... AND ME!"

"SOMEHOW, I KNOW I'M TO TAKE THE TREASURE AND HIDE IT IN THE WOODS AT THE FOOT OF THE HILL."
"DON'T ASK HOW I LUG IT ALL DOWN THERE IN ONE TRIP! IT'S ENOUGH THAT I DO."

"FROM MY HIDING PLACE I CAN SEE THE HILL AND THE DARK NIGHT SKY ABOVE--IT'S ALL SO CLEAR."
"THE NOHUMP RIDERS APPROACH THE EMPTY CART AND LOOK IT OVER."
"PUCKERNUTS! I'M JUST MOMENTS AWAY FROM BIG, BIG TROUBLE!"

"BUT NO! THE HUMANS DON'T SEEM INTERESTED AFTER ALL! THEY LEAVE..."

"...AND THEN, RIGHT OVER THE CART, HIGHER UP IN THE SKY THAN I HAVE WORDS TO TELL, THERE APPEARS A BUNCH OF VERY STRANGE STARS..."
"...SO BIG, SO BRIGHT, THEY DON'T SEEM REAL!"

"THEY START TO SWIRL ABOUT, EIGHTS UPON EIGHTS OF THEM..."
"...LOOPING AND SWOOPING LIKE A FLOCK OF BIRDS... OR LIKE WINDBLOWN, COLORED LEAVES IN THE SEASON OF DEATH-SLEEP!"
"SUDDENLY IT DAWNS ON ME-- THEY'RE ALIVE! AND THEY CAN THINK!"
"I SENSE THEY'VE COME TO TAKE SOMETHING FROM HERE... TO SOME 'WHERE' ELSE."
"WHEREVER IT IS, I WANT TO GO TOO-- SO BADLY IT HURTS!"
"OH, PLEASE... PLEASE... LET ME BE THE SOMETHING THEY MEAN TO CARRY AWAY!"

"THEY'RE LEAVING! JUST ONE LONE, LAGGARD STAR REMAINS."
NOOOOO!! DON'T GO!
IT'S ME! YOU'RE SUPPOSED TO TAKE MEEEEEE!
"THANK THE HIGH ONES! THE LAG-BEHIND STAR HEARS ME!"
"IT'S COMING DOWN! I REACH UP TO GREET IT AND..."
"...IT BEGINS TO RACE ROUND AND ROUND MY TWO HANDS, FASTER AND FASTER!"
"I FEEL A TUGGING AT MY WRISTS... PLEASANT... NOT A BIT PAINFUL!"
"AS IF I WEIGH NO MORE THAN A FEATHER, THE WHIRLING STAR PULLS ME RIGHT OFF THE GROUND!"
AAHHH HA HA HA HA HAH!

"OH! HOW CAN I TELL OF THE JOY BUBBLING OUT OF ME AS I FLOAT UP, OVER THE HILLS... OVER THE WOODS... OVER THE HUMANS' HUTS?!"
"FREE, THAT'S HOW I FEEL! FLOWN HIGH AND FAR BY A FRIENDLY STAR..."
"...I WHOOP AND SHRIEK AND LAUGH OUT LOUD LIKE I'M COMPLETELY CRAZY!"

"SUDDENLY, IT'S DAYTIME. I FLY, UNAFRAID, RIGHT DOWN TO THE HUMANS' BUSTLING HIVE."
"THEY SEE ME. AND I WANT THEM TO!"
"I HAVE GREAT FUN SURPRISING THEM, WALKING ABOUT FOR A BIT..."
"...THEN WISHING TO SOAR AWAY-- AND DOING IT..."
"...AS EASILY AS A TUFTED SEEDLING RIDES THE BREEZE."
"I'M FREE...FREE TO CONQUER THE HIGHEST, CLOUD-TOUCHING ROOFTOP THE FIVE-FINGERED ONES, IN ALL THEIR PRIDE, HAVE BUILT."
"THEN, ALL AT ONCE, THE FLIGHT IS OVER."

"I FIND MYSELF IN A ROOM, SITTING ON THE SOFT CUSHIONS OF A SLEEPING-PIT!"
"MY FRIENDLY STAR SHATTERS, SPRINKLING DOWN ON ME AS A BLANKET OF MAGIC..."
"...THAT LOOKS JUST LIKE A PLAIN, OLD, RUSTY-COLORED HIDE!"

"I TALK TO IT... CHATTERING ABOUT ALL THE CHANGES IN THE WORLD... AND IN ME. ABOUT GIVING UP MY WOLF BLOOD..."
"...ABOUT BELIEVING MY WHOLE TRIBE DEAD, ONLY TO FIND THEM-- AND MY CHIEF-FRIEND-- SO MANY TURNS OLDER THAN I REMEMBER."

TELL ME, BLANKET... WHERE DO I BELONG?
"I GUESS IT'S THE RIGHT QUESTION..."

"...BECAUSE IT GETS ME A MOST SURPRISING RESPONSE!"

"IN HER BEAUTY SHE SHIMMERS LIKE THE STAR SHE ONCE WAS."
"AND THOUGH SHE SEEMS YOUNG, THERE'S A SENSE OF GREAT AGE AND WISDOM ABOUT HER."

"WE'RE BOTH DELIGHTED TO DISCOVER EACH OTHER."

"WILL SHE ANSWER MY QUESTION?"
"WHAT?! MORE MAGIC!"
"IT-IT'S STARJUMPER...!"
"...LOOKING AT ME WITH HIS BRIGHT, BLACK EYES..."
"...WANTING TO PLAY ROUGH-AND-TUMBLE LIKE HE ALWAYS DID!"
"HE'S NOT THE ANSWER I WAS EXPECTING. BUT MAYBE..."

...MAYBE YOU'RE SUPPOSED TO LOOK TWICE!
MAYBE!
DREAMING OR AWAKE, YOU'RE AS I REMEMBER YOU, BROTHER...
...ALWAYS SOFTENING THE PATH FOR ME WITH A SMILE-- AND A DREAMBERRY HEAD TALE.
CUTTER, YOU DON'T HAVE TO...
NO. PIKE'S RIGHT.
THE GAME WILL END HOW IT ENDS...WITH ME.

CUTTER'S SO CHANGED...LOOKS LIKE A HARDENED WARRIOR.
HOW CAN HE BE SO SCARED TO SHARE HIS DREAM... NO MATTER HOW BAD IT MAY BE?
YOU ARE MY STRENGTH... ALWAYS WERE. I'VE NEVER NEEDED IT MORE!
LIFEMATE...
THIS GAME HASN'T BEEN MUCH FUN FOR SOME.
GUESS I'M GLAD IT'S ALMOST OVER.
DREAMTIME
PART 12
SQUARING HIS SHOULDERS, THE WOLFRIDER CHIEF SENDS...
...AN OPEN SENDING TO THE ENTIRE TRIBE.

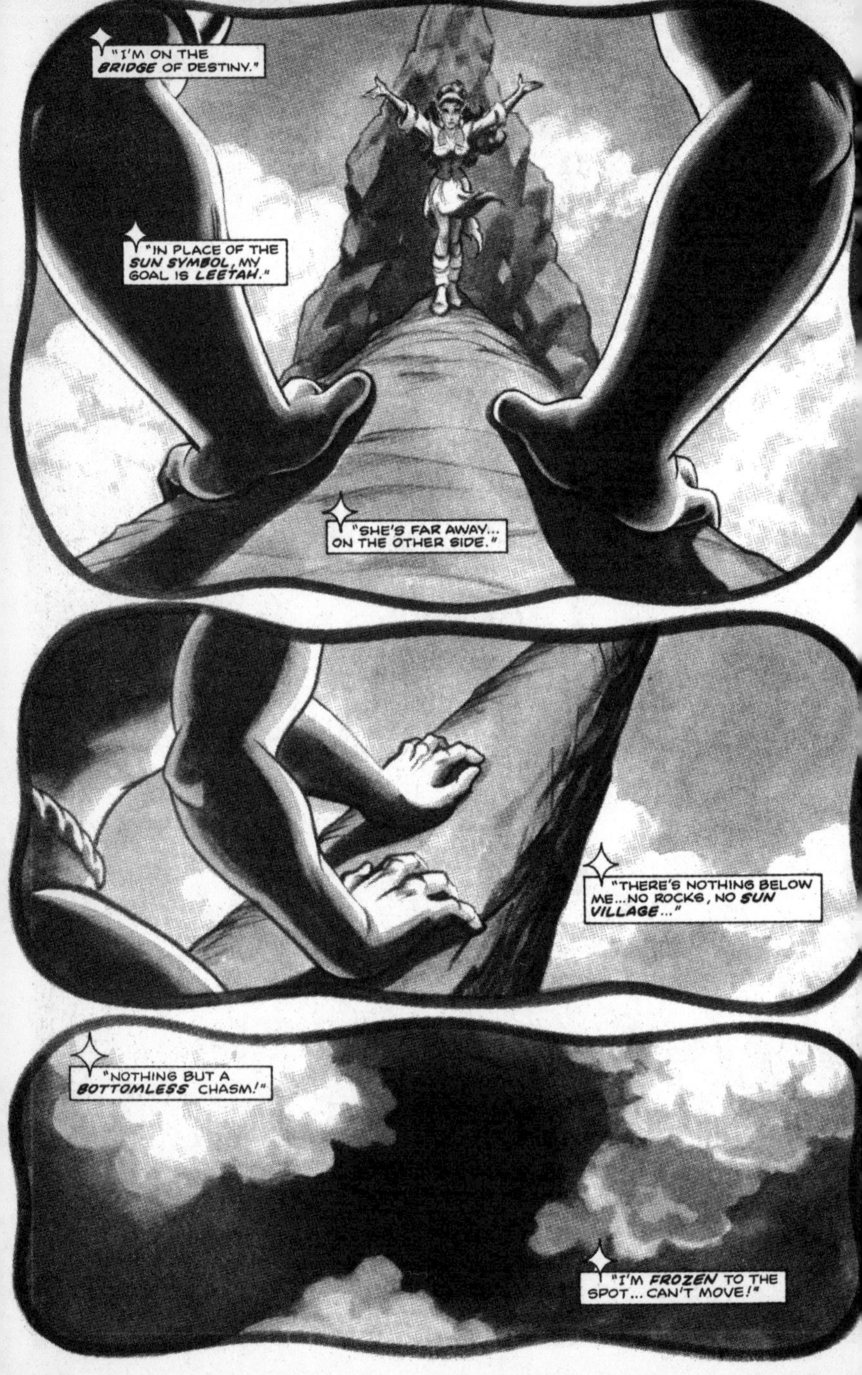
"I'M ON THE BRIDGE OF DESTINY."
"IN PLACE OF THE SUN SYMBOL, MY GOAL IS LEETAH."
"SHE'S FAR AWAY... ON THE OTHER SIDE."
"THERE'S NOTHING BELOW ME...NO ROCKS, NO SUN VILLAGE..."
"NOTHING BUT A BOTTOMLESS CHASM!"
"I'M FROZEN TO THE SPOT... CAN'T MOVE!"

"THEN, WITHOUT WARNING, HE SWEEPS HER OFF THE BRIDGE!"
"MY RIVAL... MY GREAT ENEMY... RAYEK!"
"I FALL, KNOWING I'VE FAILED HER-- FAILED EVERYONE!"
"I'VE LOST THE TRIAL OF HEAD, HAND AND HEART!"
"AND I'VE LOST SOMETHING ELSE... SOMETHING I'LL NEVER GET BACK..."
UNEXPECTEDLY, PAINFULLY, CUTTER BREAKS OFF THE SENDING...
HUH?!
ENOUGH! I'LL TAKE YOU NO FURTHER!
BELOVED...!
BUT YOUR DREAM'S NO WORSE THAN THE OTHERS, CUTTER! WHY--?
SORRY, PIKE!
IT'S NOT THE DREAM I FEAR TO SHARE...

IT'S WHAT FOLLOWS... THE COUNTING!
WHEN I FOUND MY FAMILY, I THOUGHT I'D BE HAPPY AGAIN. DIDN'T KNOW THE SADNESS WOULD STAY.
TIMMORN'S BLOOD! WHAT CAN WE DO?
LEETAH, THE CUBS AND I... WE'D GIVE ANYTHING TO MAKE IT LIKE IT WAS...
...BEFORE RAYEK...
YOU KNOW WHAT WILL HEAL YOUR HEART, BELOVED. PLEASE TELL!
THE "NOW OF WOLF THOUGHT..."
BUT IF I SEND HOW IT FEELS TO LOSE IT, THE TRIBE WILL LOSE IT TOO--
--AND THAT'LL BE THE END OF US! I'D RATHER DIE!
BUT-- BUT I...
DON'T PRESS HIM, PIKE.
DON'T SEEK A NAME FOR WHAT YOU HAVE.
IT'S TOO PRECIOUS.
THERE'S ONE ADVANTAGE. IN EXCHANGE FOR THE "NOW," I'VE GOTTEN GOOD AT LOOKING AHEAD.
AS CHIEF IN THESE NEW TIMES, IT'S A SKILL I'LL NEED PLENTY OF!
HOW DO YOU KNOW...?
HEH...
HAVEN'T YOU BEEN FOLLOWING THE DREAM GAME, YOUNGER BROTHER?

AHA!
I THOUGHT SO!
YOUR TALK ABOUT DREAMS MEANING NOTHING WAS ONLY THAT--TALK!
I KNEW IT ALL THE TIME!
SOMEHOW, WHILE WE SLEPT, THE WHOLE TRIBE CAUGHT THE SCENT OF WHAT LIES ON THE PATH BEFORE US.
SHOW HIM, PIKE.
SHOW US ALL WHAT YOU'VE FIGURED OUT!
HAH! FOR WHAT THAT'S WORTH--!
--PIKE'S ARROWS ARE MOSTLY HALF-COCKED!
BUT MY SPEAR MOSTLY HITS HOME! JUST WATCH!
AROREE... IF YOU PLEASE!
HEY! WHAT GIVES?
SPLITTING US UP...!?
I DON'T LIKE THIS!
WHAT'RE YOU TWO UP TO?
WHAT'S THE BIG IDEA, SPEAR-TOSSER?
SHENSHEN... TYLEET... YOU FIRST!
YOUR SHARED DREAM IS THE KEY TO ALL THE OTHERS!

I HOPE YOUR VISION OF ME WITH CUB COMES TRUE!
TO ME, IT SEEMS AS IF IT ALREADY HAS!
"ALREADY HAS!" THINK!
WHAT IF, WHEN WE'RE DREAMING, WE'RE REALLY LIVING AND DOING SOMEWHERE ELSE?
"IN HER SLEEP-VISION, TYLEET IS ACCEPTED BY HUMANS--AS HUMAN."
"WHEN THINGS START TO CLOSE IN ON HER, SHE'S HELPED BY THEM...LIFTED HIGH TO SEE FAR
"WHO'S TO SAY THAT ISN'T ALREADY SO...OR WON'T BE
"THINK OF OLD MAGGOTY'S WORDS IN SHENSHEN'S DREAM...
cackle cackle DREAMS NEVER HAPPEN "NOW!"
"SHENSHEN AND TYLEET SHARE A KNOWING! "NOW" MEANS "HERE AND NOW!""

"HERE"... THAT'S THE WORLD WHEN WE'RE AWAKE!
"NOW" IS ALL THERE IS WHEN WE'RE AWAKE!
AND WHAT'S BEFORE AND WHAT'S BEHIND ARE ALL ONE, RIGHT, LIFEMATES? THESE ARE VISIONS OF LIGHT!
Hmph! MY DREAM DIDN'T SEEM SO "LIGHT" TO ME!
WERE YOU SCARED?
NOT A BIT!
THAT'S WHAT I MEAN!
"LIGHT VISIONS HAVE NO FEAR IN THEM. OH, THINGS HAPPEN..."
"LIKE SO-- ZHANTEE SEES THE SUN VILLAGE WIPED OUT."
"BUT HE GOES WITH IT AND IS RAISED HIGH, LIKE TYLEET, TO SEE FAR!"
"SAME WITH VENKA. SHE FLIES ABOVE THE FIRE AND ICE WARRING FOR HER LOYALTY."
"BUT SHE LIFTS HERSELF!"

"AND DO WE NEED TO TALK ABOUT SKYWISE'S DREAM?!"
EEEEYOOWW HOO HOOO HA HA
chuckle
WHAT ABOUT YOURS! WHEN YOUR SURROUNDINGS CLOSED IN ON YOU--
"--YOU DIDN'T EXACTLY RISE ABOVE 'EM!"
NOPE... BUT I WASN'T SCARED!
FLYING HIGH OR CREEPING LOW, YOU STILL SEE FARTHER THAN WHEN YOU'RE IN THE THICK OF THINGS!
AND "IN THE THICK OF THINGS" IS WHERE MOST WOLFRIDERS TEND TO LIVE!
THAT'S CERTAIN! NOW... FOR THE DARK STUFF! JUST REMEMBER...
...DREAMS NEVER HAPPEN NOW!

REDLANCE, THIS GAME BEGAN WITH YOUR DREAM.
IT EEMED SO REAL. ARE OU SAYING T COULD BE?
TREESTUMP... DID YOURS FEEL REAL?
THE FEAR AND GUILT, YES. BUT WHAT I DID... NO!
YOU'RE BOTH RIGHT!
"YOU BOTH SAW THE FOREST SHRINK. REDLANCE WAS THE HELPLESS FATHER TREE, DESTROYED BY HUMANS WITH METAL TOOLS AND WEAPONS!"
"AND TREESTUMP WAS POWERLESS TO KEEP HIS OWN METAL WEAPONS FROM KILLING WHAT HE LOVES MOST!"

YOU ALL SHARE A KNOWING ABOUT THINGS LONG LOST... LIKE THE HOLT.
NIGHT-FALL AND TREESTUMP'S DREAMS WARN--
"--THAT SOME OF US MAY BE AS MUCH TO BLAME AS THE HUMANS IF WE LOSE IT AGAIN!"
"BUT THEN, IF YOU THINK ABOUT IT, ALL OUR DREAMS ARE ABOUT THINGS CLOSING IN ON US."
"STRONGBOW AND MOONSHADE KNOW DEEPEST...FORGIVING--AND LETTING BE--IS SOMETIMES ALL WE CAN DO."

THEN, MY DREAM--OF THE PIT--THOUGH IT'S DIFFERENT FROM MEMORY... IS TRUE?
ALL DREAMS ARE TRUE...EVEN ONES THAT SEEM BACKWARDS FROM WHAT REALLY HAPPENS!
THE "KNOWING" IN US KNOWS ALL SIDES!
SO, WHAT IF DREAM TIME SPILLS INTO AWAKE TIME?
YEAH! HOW COME HALF OF US HAD GOOD DREAMS, AND THE OTHER HALF BAD?
Hmmm... WELL, HALF OF US CAN LIVE FOREVER!
"THE HALF THAT CAN'T HAS FEAR-DREAMS--SORT OF LIKE 'KEEP ALIVE' PRACTICE."
BUT THOSE LIKE PIKE AND TYLEET, WHO THINK AS IMMORTALS, ARE SIMPLY FREE OF FEAR.
THINGS DIE, THEY'RE REBORN AND THEY DIE AGAIN IN ENDLESS TURNINGS.
I THINK OUR DREAMS SAY NOTHING LASTS FOREVER --EXCEPT SPIRIT.
HIGH ONE...

WOLFRIDERS! WE'RE AWAKE! WE KNOW WHAT WE KNOW!
THE WORLD HAS CHANGED, AND OUR SMALL, GREEN PATCH OF IT WILL GET SMALLER!
BUT THERE'S POWER IN KNOWING! IF THIS HOLT FALLS, WE WON'T!
ON MY HEART I SWEAR THERE WILL ALWAYS BE A FATHER TREE, HERE, NOW, AND IN OUR DREAMS!
OOO
WWOOOOOO

REMEMBER THIS, KITLINGS. ***THIS*** IS THE STRENGTH YOU COME FROM.

AND THAT IS YOUR SIRE, WHO LOVED US... AND NEVER FORGOT US... FOR ***EIGHT EIGHTS*** TIMES ***EIGHT*** TURNS OF SEASON.

DAWN'S FIRST, THIN RAYS DELICATELY SPECKLE THE TOWERING TREES OF ***THORNY MOUNTAIN HOLT.***

THE FOREST AWAKENS TO A CHORUS OF BIRDSONG AND THE CHATTER OF SMALL, FURRY SEED-SEEKERS.

WITH THE WOODLAND DAY'S ORDINARY BUSINESS BEGUN, THE COUNCIL OF WOLFRIDERS ENDS...

GLAD YOU STUCK TO IT, SQUIRREL-CHEEKS!
UM, Heh Heh...
A NEW KIND OF HEALING! I'VE LEARNED MUCH!
YOU MUST HELP PIKE KEEP ALL OUR DREAMS FROM NOW ON, AROREE...

"...AND YOURS TOO, FOR YOU SHALL HAVE DREAMS OF YOUR OWN AGAIN, I PROMISE!"
WHO'D EVER GUESS PIKE WOULD COME UP WITH A GAME THAT WOULD WEAR OUT OUR THINK-MUSCLES?!
Yawn ...EYES WON'T STAY OPEN!

"BET NO FEAR-DREAMS COME CALLING ON US WHEN WE'RE THIS TIRED!"
AAAAAAAAAAAAAAAH!
¡gasp¡
ONE... ...TWO... ...THREE... ...FOUR...
"ALL DREAMS ARE TRUE...THE KNOWING IN US KNOWS ALL SIDES!" WHAT THE WOLF CHIEF KNOWS IS THAT THE DREAM-GAME IS OVER-- FOR EVERYONE BUT HIM.

For ten thousand
years the
World of Two Moons
went on as the
Wolfriders dreamed.

And while they
were sleeping...

FOR TEN THOUSAND YEARS, THE ELVES SLEEP.
IN TEN THOUSAND YEARS, MUCH CAN HAPPEN.
THE PRICE OF A SOUL
THE HALFLING KNOWN AS TWO-EDGE HAS WAITED ALL HIS LIFE FOR THE MOMENT HE FEELS NOW DRAWING CLOSE.
THE RESONANCE WITHIN HIS BRAIN IS STRONG NOW. THE HEALING, SOOTHING INFLUENCE OF LEETAH HAS CALMED HIS RAGING SOUL--
--AT LEAST A LITTLE.
ENOUGH TO LET HIM FOCUS ON THE CRADLE OF HIS PAIN.

ENOUGH TO LET HIM BRING TO LIFE, AT LAST, THE VENGEANCE HE HAS SCHEMED UPON FOR YEARS BE-YOND NUMBERING.
GOOD EVENING, MOTHER.

IT WAS YOU, WASN'T IT? YOU WHO I FELT IN MY MIND.
IT WAS YOUR TOUCH THAT BROUGHT ME HERE.
YES. THIS ELVEN GIFT OF SENDING HAS OPENED A NEW WORLD TO ME.
I CAN TRACK THE MINDS OF OTHERS--AS I TRACKED YOURS.
AND I CAN TOUCH THE MINDS OF OTHERS, AS I TOUCHED YOURS.
SAVE YOUR STRENGTH, MOTHER.
MY LITTLE TRAP WAS BUILT WITH ONLY YOU IN MIND. IT KNOWS YOUR TRICKS.
IT WAS NOT ENOUGH TO SIMPLY FOLLOW YOU, AS YOU MOVED BENEATH THE OCEANS, MOTHER.
FOR MY PLAN TO SUCCEED, I NEEDED TO LURE YOU TO THIS PLACE.
AND HAVING ACCOMPLISHED THIS..?
WHAT IS YOUR PLEASURE NOW, TWO-EDGE?

I OWE YOU A DEBT, MOTHER.
SOME TIME AGO, YOU GAVE ME SHELTER.
IT IS NOW MY WISH TO REPAY THAT DEBT.
IN KIND!

GOOD MORNING, MOTHER.
DID YOU SLEEP WELL?

NO.
BUT, WAS THAT NOT YOUR INTENT?
I DO NOT WISH UPON YOU UNNECESSARY HARDSHIP, MOTHER.
NOT ONE BIT MORE, IN FACT, THAN YOU PLACED UPON ME.
I AM TO BE MADE TO SUFFER, AS I MADE YOU SUFFER.
HOW SMALL OF YOU, TWO-EDGE.
DESPITE YOUR MANY OTHER SHORTCOMINGS, I HAD ALWAYS THOUGHT YOU BIGGER THAN THAT.
I AM.
BUT YOU TAUGHT ME WELL, MOTHER. YOU TAUGHT ME FEAR, AND YOU TAUGHT ME HATE.
AS YOU MADE ME SUFFER FOR THE CRIME OF MY EXISTENCE.

ALL THAT I AM, I AM BECAUSE OF YOU, MOTHER.
BECAUSE YOU WERE CURIOUS.
"BECAUSE YOUR CRUELTY COMPELLED YOU TO SEDUCE A TROLL.
"MY FATHER.
"AND WHEN I WAS BORN, YOU SAW IN ME NOTHING MORE THAN A BLANK CANVAS...
"...ON WHICH TO WORK YOUR EVIL MAGIC.
"I WAS HALF ELF, HALF TROLL...
"...BUT YOU WOULD SEE TO IT THAT I COULD NEVER BE COMPLETELY EITHER.
YOU ARE A HEALER, MOTHER.
THE GREATEST HEALER OF THEM ALL. GREATER EVEN THAN LEETAH.
BUT YOU PERVERT YOUR GIFT. USE IT TO CAUSE PAIN...

...INSTEAD OF CURE IT.
WITH ONE TOUCH OF YOUR MIND YOU COULD HAVE STILLED THE FURIES THAT TEAR APART MY SOUL.
INSTEAD, IT AMUSED YOU TO REACH INTO MY BRAIN AND MAKE THINGS WORSE.
BUT... I AM A MOST INATTENTIVE HOST.
YOU MUST BE HUNGRY...
HERE...
I HAVE BROUGHT YOU SOME BREAK-FAST.
AH-GH!
MISERABLE CRAWLING DUNGBALL!
THAT YOU SHOULD HAVE SPRUNG FROM MY WOMB...!

AGAIN I ADVISE YOU TO CONSERVE YOUR ENERGIES, DEAR MOTHER.
I CAN FEEL YOU, INSIDE MY MIND. BUT I AM ARMORED AGAINST YOU, NOW.
I HAVE SPENT YEARS TRAINING MYSELF TO RESIST YOUR POWER.
DO YOU HONESTLY THINK I WOULD EVEN HAVE ATTEMPTED TO CAPTURE AND HOLD YOU, WERE THAT NOT THE CASE?
AND NOW, I HAVE MANY THINGS TO ATTEND TO.
I WILL BID YOU GOOD DAY, MOTHER.
"WE WILL TALK AGAIN TOMORROW."
WE WILL DO MORE THAN TALK, TWO-EDGE.
ARMORED YOU MAY THINK YOU ARE, AGAINST MY POWER...
...BUT YOU HAVE STUCK YOUR FAT NOSE INTO A PLACE YOU CANNOT EVEN START TO UNDERSTAND.
THINK YOURSELF A MATCH FOR WINNOWILL, DO YOU?
IGNORANT SLUG! YOUR PRISONER I MAY BE, FOR NOW...
...BUT I'LL NOT SLEEP UNTIL...
SLEEP..!

OF COURSE!
ARMORED YOU MAY THINK YOU ARE, TWO-EDGE...
"...BUT THERE IS ONE PLACE IN WHICH ALL MINDS ARE OPEN.
"ONE PLACE YOU CANNOT HIDE YOURSELF FROM THE POWER OF WINNOWILL..."
HURH..?
WHERE..?
TWO-EDGE!
WHAT? SOMEONE... SENDING TO ME.
TWO-EDGE!
HERE! I'M OVER HERE!

LEETAH..?
YES, TWO-EDGE. I AM HERE.
I AM HERE FOR YOU.
N-NO! THIS IS NOT RIGHT. YOU ARE CUTTER'S MATE.
BUT CUTTER IS NOT HERE.
DO NOT BE AFRAID, SWEET TWO-EDGE.
I BRING YOU THE GIFT FOR WHICH YOU HAVE LONGED.
LEETAH'S POWER HAS HEALED YOU IN THE PAST.
LET IT WORK UPON YOU NOW.
LET IT SET YOU FREE.

TROLL YOU ARE, TWO-EDGE.
BUT ELF, ALSO.
TOGETHER WE RELEASE THE BEAUTY YOU HAVE SO LONG KEPT LOCKED IN UGLINESS.
IN OUR JOINING YOU ARE MADE WHOLE.
BUT... HOW?
LEETAH...
MY HANDS...
WHAT...
YOU HAVE ALWAYS HELD WITHIN YOU THE KEY TO YOUR OWN PRISON, TWO-EDGE.
FOR LOVE, TWO-EDGE.
YOU HAD BUT TO LET YOURSELF REACH OUT FOR THAT WHICH YOU MOST DESIRED.
MY LOVE.
A MOTHER'S LOVE.

NO-OOOHH!!
WITCH!
DEVIL!
WILL YOU NEVER BE CONTENT?
NOT UNTIL I AM DRIVEN MAD..?!?
DONE?? DONE??
WHAT HAVE YOU NOT DONE??
REACHING INTO MY MIND, TORTURING ME WITH MY OWN DREAMS!
BUT NO MORE! NO MORE!!
AND WHAT HAVE I DONE, TWO-EDGE, THAT WAS SO TERRIBLE..?
THE WATER ..?

YES! DRAINING AWAY!
CAN YOU CHANGE YOUR SHAPE FAST ENOUGH TO KEEP FROM DROWNING, MOTHER?
YOU KNOW I CAN'T.
WHAT..??
BEFORE, YOU SPOKE OF DEBTS TO BE REPAID.
IS THIS HOW YOU REPAY ME FOR GRANTING YOU YOUR FONDEST WISH?
LOOK AT YOURSELF, TWO-EDGE!
THERE WAS MORE TO YOUR DREAM THAN YOU GUESSED!
NO..!!
HOW..?!?

YOU ARE MY SON, TWO-EDGE.
AND THOUGH MY POWERS ARE DILUTED BY YOUR TROLL BLOOD...
...YOU SHARE THEM, SHARE MY ABILITIES.
THE POWER TO ALTER YOUR FORM... HAS ALWAYS BEEN... WITHIN YOU, TWO-EDGE.
DENIED TO YOU... ONLY BY YOUR OWN DENIAL OF... YOUR ELVEN HERITAGE.
ACCEPT IT, TWO-EDGE. ACCEPT... THE PART OF YOU... THAT COMES FROM ME...
...AND ALL... THESE WONDERS AND... DELIGHTS ARE YOURS.
HERE... IS MY MOTHER'S GIFT TO YOU... TWO-EDGE.
YOU HAVE... BUT TO ACCEPT... YOUR TRUE NATURE... AND IT WILL... BE...
...YOURS...

FAR BENEATH THE OCEAN'S WAVES, WHERE THE LIGHT OF THE TWO MOONS DOES NOT REACH...
...MOVING SWIFT AND SILENT THROUGH THE ETERNAL DARK-- WINNOWILL.
TWO-EDGE HAS MADE HIS DECISION, AND IN SO DOING, SET HIS MOTHER FREE.
SHE WONDERS, SINCE HE CAN FEEL HER MIND, IF HE CAN SENSE HER LAUGHTER.
ELSEWHERE...
TWO MOONS LOOK DOWN UPON THE ROCKY SHORE. THEIR PALLID LIGHT BRINGS NO WARMTH TO THE NIGHT.
AND FAR BELOW, IN A CHAMBER HEWN FROM THE LIVING ROCK, THERE IS NO LIGHT AT ALL, ONLY DARKNESS AND COLD.
DARKNESS AND COLD THAT CROWD IN CLOSE AROUND A HUDDLED FIGURE, SMALL AND SILENT IN THE VAST WOMB OF THE EARTH.
HE DOES NOT MIND THE DARKNESS, FOR IT HIDES HIM. HE DOES NOT FEEL THE COLD, FOR THERE IS A COLDER PLACE INSIDE HIM.
IN THE HEART OF A TROLL CALLED TWO-EDGE.

GOING BACK

THERE..! THE HOLE RAYEK DUG TO BAR US GO-BACKS FROM OUR LODGE!

"HOLE"?! WITH THAT MUCH MAGIC IN HIM, NO WONDER HE WAS ABLE TO SPIRIT THE PALACE INTO ANOTHER TIME!

YOU MAY BE CHIEF OF A TRIBE THAT NO LONGER EXISTS, BELOV...EH...KAHVI.

BAH! A LITTLE TRENCH LIKE THAT COULDN'T THWART *MY* WARRIOR-FOLK LONG, *TYLDAK!*
IT'S HONEST BRAGGING I'VE DONE ON THEM ALL THESE CRUSTINGS. WAIT AND SEE!

BUT WE SEND AND SEND...AND NO ANSWER COMES!

TWOINNNG!

>GASP!<
HIGH ONES!!

ROTTEN, POKING *TROLL!*
!?!

HOLD IT, YOU!

TRY TO MAIM *MY* BEAUTIFUL BIRD, WILL YOU?! LET'S IMPROVE *YOUR* FACE...

AAARRRRooooooo

....

WELL! SURPRISED LOOKS ON NEW FACES I CAN UNDERSTAND...
BUT YOU, VOK, AND CHEIDER... MARDU... KIV... YOU'D BEST CLOSE YOUR MOUTHS BEFORE YOUR TONGUES FREEZE TO YOUR BOTTOM TEETH!
!?!
???
!!!
HERE! WHAT'S THIS, ROFF... TROLL MEAT?! I THOUGHT WE GAVE THAT UP RIGHT AFTER WE WON THE PALACE WAR!
K-KAHVI..?!
IT'S KAHVI! OUR KAHVI! SHE'S RETURNED!!
THAT'S MORE LIKE IT! VOK, MY OLD FUR WARMER, WHY DIDN'T YOU RETURN MY SENDINGS?
I-I GUESS... I'M OUT OF PRACTICE!
>CHOKE< SHE DIDN'T DIE IN SOME FORSAKEN PLACE! ISN'T IT WONDROUS, CHIEF ZEY?
INDEED!
WE MUST DO WHAT WE CAN TO MAKE THIS SUDDENLY LIVING LEGEND WELCOME!

...DON'T ASK ME HOW! RAYEK TOOK THE PALACE TO SOME FAR-AHEAD TIME, THAT'S ALL I KNOW! THERE WAS NO WAY TO GIVE CHASE... NO WAY TO CLAIM REVENGE.

MY DAUGHTER AND I LIVED IN THE NEW LAND WITH THE WOLFRIDERS...WAITING. BUT THE PALACE NEVER CAME BACK.

FINALLY, WHEN VENKA WAS GROWN, TYLDAK AND I SOUGHT THE FROZEN MOUNTAINS TOGETHER. IT TOOK A LONG TIME. THE WOLFRIDER CHIEF WAS RIGHT. I MISSED YOU ALL.

ALL WHO KNEW YOU MANY CRUSTINGS AGO, YOU MEAN!

WE DANCED FOR YOU ALL RIGHT, SANG YOU PRAISE-FILLED DEATHSONGS.

BUT AS IT TURNS OUT...YOU FAILED THE PALACE...

...MAY BE GONE FOR GOOD! AYE! MEANTIME, YOU'VE LET YOURSELVES SINK LOWER THAN TROLLS! THAT'S YOUR FAULT, ZEY!
WHAT HAPPENED TO URDA? I LEFT HER IN CHARGE!
TROLLS AMBUSHED HER HUNTING PARTY...TOOK THEM ALL UNDERGROUND. WE GOT EVEN.
THAT'S HOW IT'S BEEN. AND THAT'S ALL THERE IS. WHAT DID YOU EXPECT?
"WE'RE GO-BACKS WITH NOTHING TO GO BACK TO...EVER...FROM WHAT YOU SAY."
OH..?
AND HOW WOULD IT BE IF I TOLD YOU I KNOW WHERE TO LAY HANDS ON A PIECE OF THE PALACE...
THE ONLY PIECE LEFT IN THE WORLD?
.........!
WHERE..? WH-WHERE...
NEVER YOU MIND! GIVE ME PROVISIONS, A COUPLE OF SHARP HUNTERS, AND FIGHTING STAGS FIT FOR A ROUGH TREK.
WE'LL BE BACK BEFORE THE NEW-GREEN FADES.
FAIR ENOUGH?
A QUEST! A REAL QUEST! COUNT ME IN!
AND ME...OUT! LEAVE THE FROZEN MOUNTAINS? NOT EVEN FOR A PIECE OF THE PALACE!

"BETTER TO STAY HERE AND DEAL WITH THE ENEMIES WE KNOW!"

DON'T TRY TO SEND, CHOT. I KNOW IT'S A STRAIN.
JUST TAKE THIS IN...

I DON'T THINK KAHVI IS LYING.
I THINK SHE MAY EVEN SUCCEED. THAT WILL MAKE HER A HERO.

AND WHAT WILL THAT MAKE ME...
...OR YOU, MY FRIEND?

DISAPPOINTED?
THEY'VE LOST SOMETHING...PRIDE, GUTS, HEART MAYBE...I DON'T KNOW. THEY NEED RAISING UP.
THEY NEED THE PALACE.

IT'S YOU THEY NEED... AS DO I.
FOOLISH BIRD! NOTHING'S SPECIAL ABOUT ME! ALL I CAN DO IS FETCH THE GO-BACKS THE LAST SCRAP OF WHAT THEY LIVED...AND DIED FOR! IT'S THEIR RIGHT!
AND I CAN ONLY STAND BY YOU...

"...DEFEND YOU...EVEN FROM YOURSELF."
WELL, CHOT... YUN... YOU WERE RUNNY-NOSED AND BARE-RUMPED LAST TIME I SAW YOU!
LET'S SEE WHAT YOU'RE MADE OF NOW!
DAYS LATER, FAR AHEAD OF HIS MUCH SLOWER TRAVELING COMPANIONS, TYLDAK CIRCLES ABOVE THE GIGANTIC, BAROQUE BURIAL MOUND WHICH WAS ONCE HIS HOME...BLUE MOUNTAIN.

REEVOL'S BOND BIRD, FROM THE LOOK OF THE HARNESS... THOUGH THERE'S LITTLE ENOUGH LEFT BY WHICH TO JUDGE.
THE BODIES OF MY PEOPLE WERE CRUSHED BENEATH THESE ROCKS. THEIR SPIRITS FLEW TO THE PALACE OF THE HIGH ONES.
WHAT PART OF THEM REMAINS WITHIN THE TINY RELIC WE SEEK, I WONDER...?
SKAAAAAWWW!
SKAAAAAAWWWWW!!
KUREEL'S SECOND FLEDGLING... MANY YEARS GROWN! AND WITH YOUNG, BY THEIR MARKINGS...
YES, YOU REMEMBER ME! YOU'VE KEPT AS CLOSE TO YOUR OLD AERIES AS YOU COULD!
BRED TO SERVE! LET'S HOPE YOU'VE PASSED THE GLIDERS' TRAINING ON TO YOUR CHICKS!

ELSEWHERE...
I HARDLY REMEMBER RAYEK...
BUT HE LEFT WISPS OF TALES THAT ALWAYS MADE ME WONDER.
ARE YOU SURE THE SUN FOLK WILL FIGHT, KAHVI?
WOULDN'T YOU? THEY'RE NOT THE SOFTLINGS THEY USED TO BE. THE VILLAGE IS SEEDED WITH WOLFRIDERS!
WE'LL TRY STEALTH FIRST AND, FAILING THAT, WE'LL SCARE 'EM GOOD! IF THEY'RE SMART THEY'LL GIVE UP BEFORE ANY BLOOD IS SHED.
I HOPE SO!
BUT THERE MAY BE AN EVEN BIGGER FIGHT WHEN WE RETURN TO THE LODGE! ZEY LIKES BEING CHIEF...VERY, VERY MUCH AND...
LOOK!
THREE GREAT HAWKS! TYLDAK'S BROUGHT THEM JUST AS YOU SAID HE WOULD, KAHVI!
AH, CHOT! MY WINGED FRIEND WOULD BRING ME BOTH MOONS IF I CHARGED HIM TO!
WE'LL BE A WHILE LEARNING TO STEER THOSE OVERFED SHRIEK-OWLS...

"...BUT THE SUN FOLK AREN'T GOING ANYWHERE! THEY'RE ROOTED DEEP AS THE RABBIT FODDER THEY GROW IN THEIR GARDENS!"

SEE! THE TIME OF FLOOD AND FLOWER! DESERT GOWNED IN COLORS BRIGHT!

RAINBOW VEILED, HER SKY BLUE BROW! HER BLOSSOMS SWEETLY SCENT THE NIGHT!

WHA..?! OH! ≥GIGGLE≤ WINDKIN!
FOLLOW ME TO YOUR PLACE OF HONOR, BEHTIA! YOU STAND FOR ALL WE CELEBRATE!
RECOGNITION AT FESTIVAL! SAME TIME, TWO YEARS LATER, A CUB! THAT HASN'T HAPPENED SINCE... SINCE WHO KNOWS?
POF!
POF!
POF!
SAVAH, THE MOTHER OF MEMORY, HAS LIT THE LANTERNS! THE NEW GREEN'S SPROUTED, THE HARVEST FOLLOWS!
SING AND DANCE FOR JOY!
HA HA HA HA! SOON AS YOU MOVE OFF THE MAT, TRY AND STOP US, DART!

AS THE NIGHT REELS ONWARD AND THE STARS BEGIN TO FADE, THE REVELRY GROWS, IF ANYTHING, EVEN MORE BOISTEROUS.

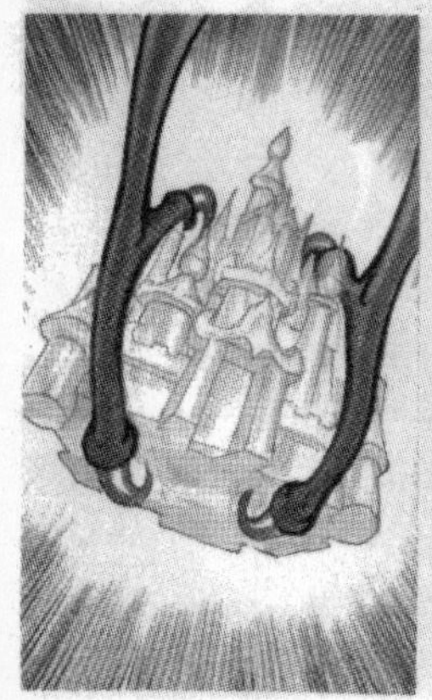

FORTUNATELY, THOUGH DAZED BY DREAMBERRY JUICE, SCOUTER CHOOSES THAT MOMENT TO LOOK UP...

...AND A FRENZY OF A DIFFERENT SORT SEIZES THE VILLAGERS.
WHO...WHAT IS IT?!
STOP!!
NO, DART! WOUND HIM AND HE MAY DROP THE LITTLE PALACE!
TYLDAK! I THOUGHT WE WERE DONE WITH HIM!

!?!

YOU! I FORGOT!

SO YOU'RE MY SIRE.
I'VE TRIED TO THINK WELL OF YOU...'TIL NOW.

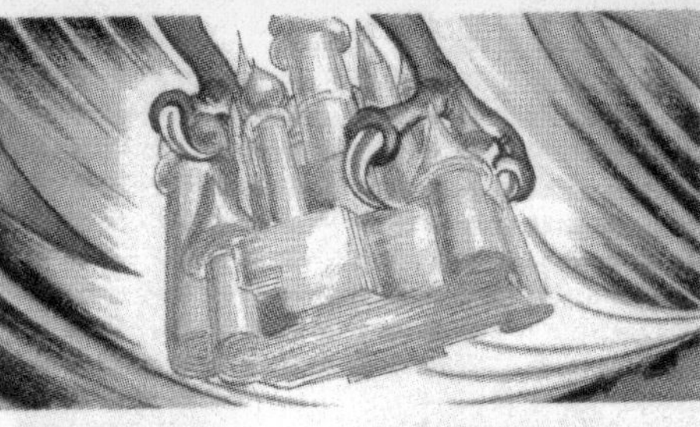

HE IS AS I WAS BEFORE I RECEIVED MY WINGS...
...LACKING SPEED, OR HEIGHT. YET, LOOK HOW FIERCELY HE PURSUES!
WAIT!!

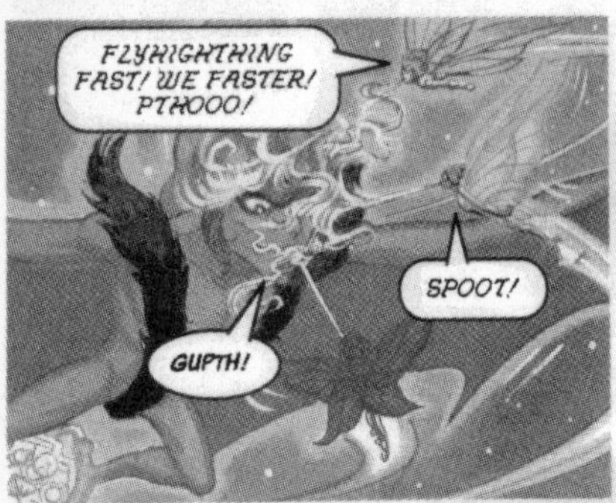
FLYHIGHTHING FAST! WE FASTER! PTHOOO!
SPOOT!
GUPTH!

>GASP!<
>GAG<
>COUGH COUGH<

WHEW!

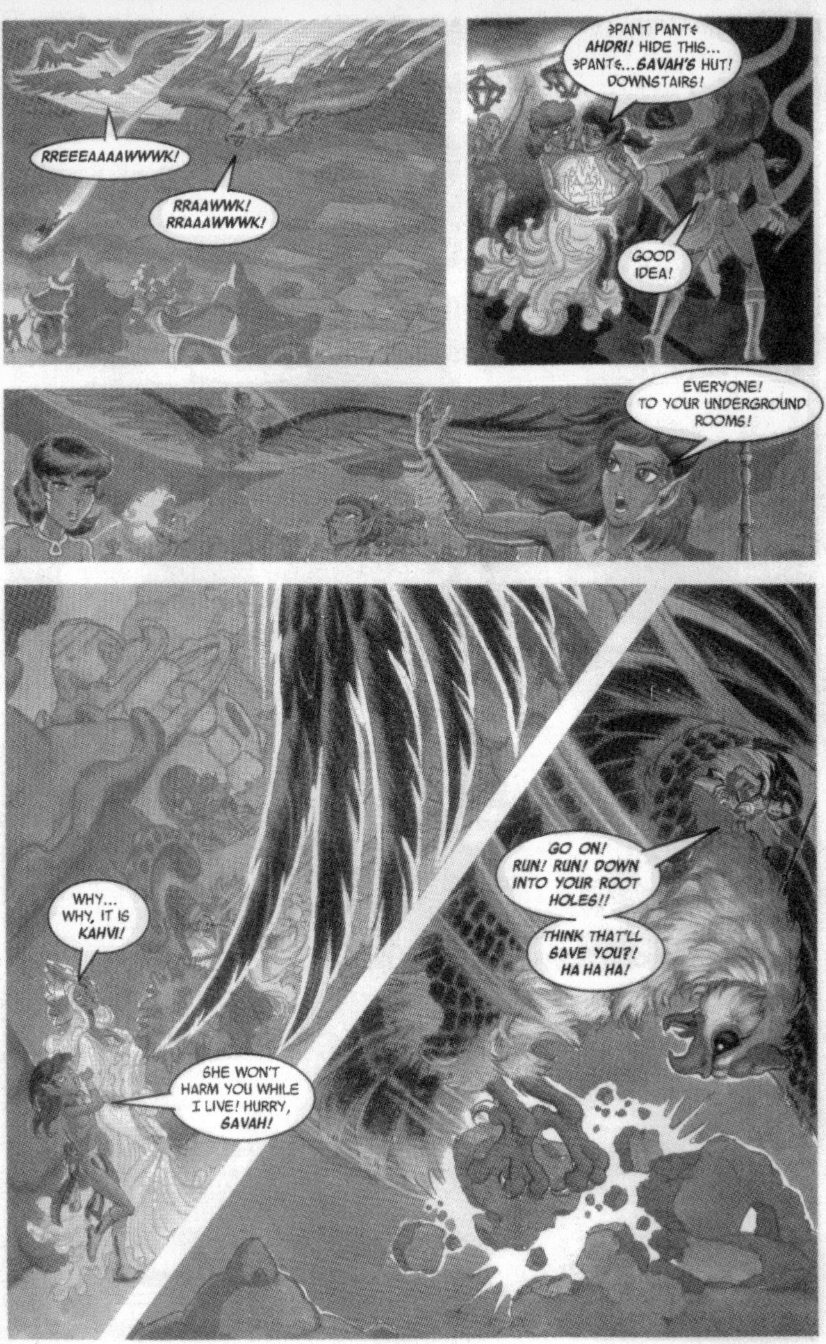

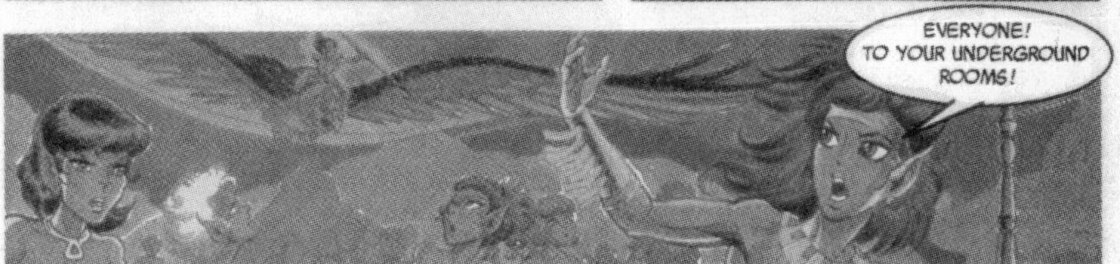

WHY... WHY, IT IS **KAHVI!**

GO ON! RUN! RUN! DOWN INTO YOUR ROOT HOLES!!

THINK THAT'LL SAVE YOU?! HA HA HA!

SHE WON'T HARM YOU WHILE I LIVE! HURRY, **SAVAH!**

THEY CALL THESE LODGES?! WE CAN RIP THE LIDS RIGHT OFF THESE CLAY POTS, EASY!
TOO BAD! I HOPE THE SUN FOLK SURRENDER QUICKLY!
HEAR ME, DESERT DWELLERS!
WE WANT BUT ONE THING, AND THAT YOU KNOW!
HAND IT OVER AND WE GO IN PEACE! REFUSE, AND IT'S YOUR GARDENS...THEN...

"...YOUR WELL!"
!#*$*!! SHE'S WEAKENING THE ROOF WITH BOULDERS! BUT SHE'LL HAVE TO DISMOUNT TO GET AT US! THEN IT'S HAND TO HAND!
DO NOT FEAR FOR ME, WING! I AM ONE JAR THAT WILL NOT LOSE ITS LID UNTIL IT IS TIME!
SELF BLAME, CHILD? WHY IN THE WORLD..?
SCOUTER IS MY FATHER, BUT TYLDAK'S MY BLOOD!
AND HE'S HELPING TO DESTROY OUR HOME! OUR BEAUTIFUL HOME..!
I-I CAN'T LET...
WOA!! THE UPPER DOME'S FALLEN THROUGH!
NO!!
WINDKIN! DON'T... OOWWW!!

HMH! THE LAD SEEKS TO LURE US AWAY FROM THE VILLAGE!
TAKE HIM UP ON IT, BEAUTIFUL BIRD! THESE HAWKS AREN'T MADE FOR DELICATE MANEUVERS!

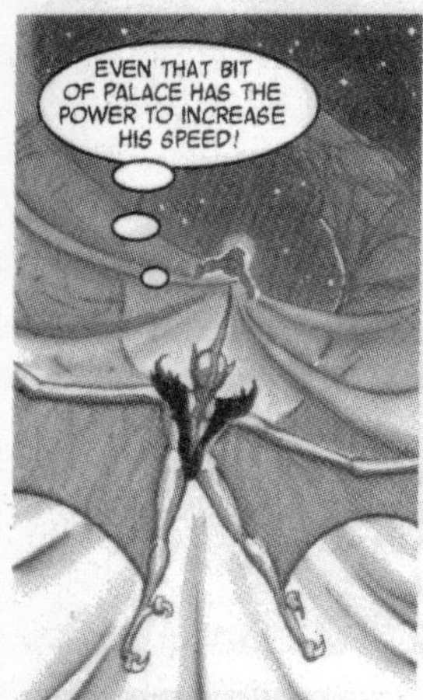
EVEN THAT BIT OF PALACE HAS THE POWER TO INCREASE HIS SPEED!

BUT NOT ENOUGH!

HUH?!

HERE! IT IS YOURS!
>SIGH< THAT'S IT, THEN! CHOT! YUN! LET'S GO!
ARROGANT! SHE RIDES WITHOUT A HALTER LOOP!

ALL THE BETTER FOR ME!

?!!

KAHVI!!

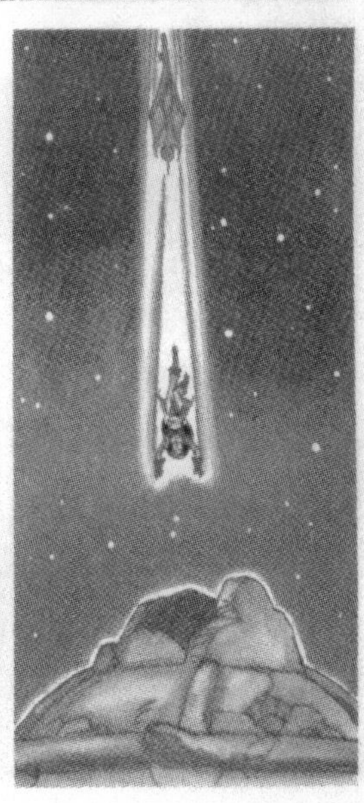

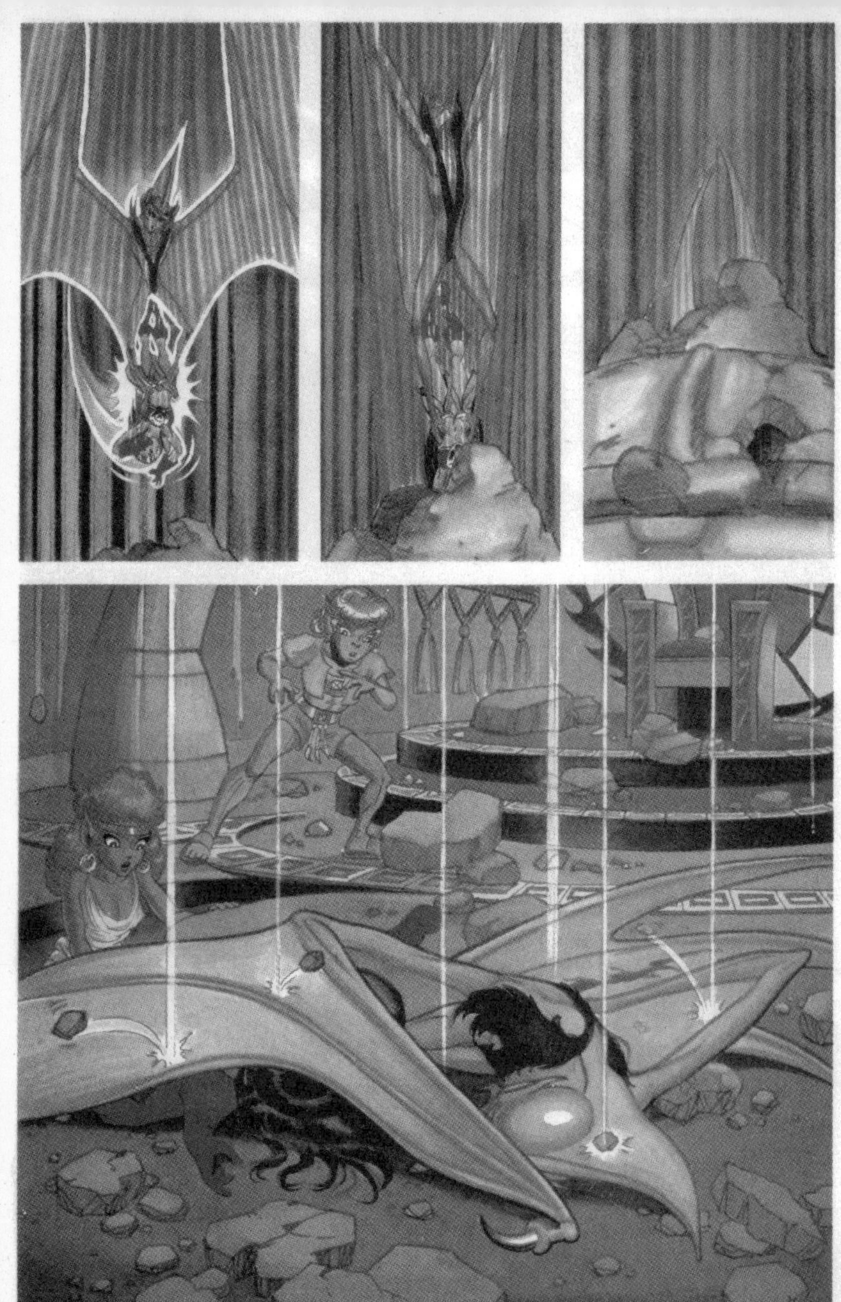

HELLO!
HELLO NICE
FLYHIGHTHING!
⋟PANT PANT PANT⋞
WHERE WERE YOU THREE?!
LOOK! THEY'VE GOT THE
LITTLE PALACE!

⋟GASP GASP⋞
I'M THROUGH! AFTER
THEM, PRESERVERS!
FLY!!

HURRY! HURRY!
NASTYBAD
HIGHTHINGS!

ZEY AND YOU...
PLANNED THIS, CHOT? IT STINKS!
WE CAN'T LEAVE KAHVI AND TYLDAK
BACK THERE!
THE PALACE...
WAIT 'TIL YOU HOLD
IT IN YOUR ARMS! THERE'S
NO FEELING LIKE IT!

ON THE OTHER
HAND...I THINK
I'LL KEEP IT
TO MYSELF!
THE ONE
WHO BRINGS IT TO
THE GO-BACK...ONLY
HE DESERVES TO
BE CHIEF!

HIGHTHING
DO RIGHT THING!

HIGHTHING
DO RIGHT THING!

HIGHTHING
DO RIGHT THING!

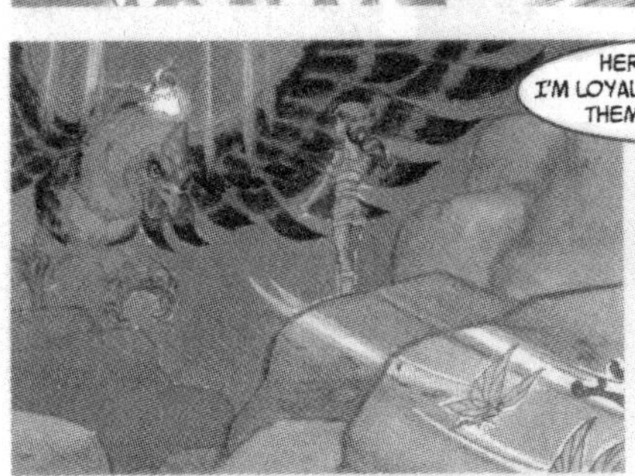

KAHVI...TYLDAK... WE ARE RELIEVED, THANKS TO ***MENDER,*** THAT YOU SURVIVED YOUR FALL.

BUT WHAT ARE YOU TO DO WITH US NOW, EH... NOW THAT THE LITTLE PALACE IS YOURS AGAIN?

YOU DAREN'T RELEASE US! IN THE GO-BACKS' NAME, WE'LL KEEP FIGHTING TO RECLAIM WHAT'S OURS!

ONE WAY OR ANOTHER WE'LL MAKE THINGS VERY MESSY FOR YOU!

IT HAS EVER BEEN MY BELIEF THAT ALL ELVES, EVEN WARRIORS, WANT PEACE ABOVE ALL. WE CANNOT GIVE YOU THE RELIC...
...BUT WE CAN INVITE THE GO-BACKS TO DWELL HERE, AS SOME OF THE WOLFRIDERS DO. WE HAVE THE ROOM, AND THE LOVE.

PTOO!

KAHVI... YOUR OWN TRIBESMAN BETRAYED YOU.
PERHAPS IT'S WISEST, AFTER ALL, TO FORGET THE GO-BACKS. THEY'RE NOT WORTH...

...IT'S WORTH MY LIFE TO RAISE THEM UP TO WHAT THEY WERE! UNDERSTAND?
HOWEVER THEY SEE ME NOW, I WAS THEIR CHIEF. AND THEY'RE MY PEOPLE!

GIVE US HALF, THEN!

HALF?! HERE! TAKE HALF MY HEAD OR HALF MY CHEST!

THE LITTLE PALACE HELPS US KEEP TRACK OF OUR BLOOD KIN ACROSS THE SEA...YOU *KNOW* THAT! BREAK IT IN TWO OVER MY COLD CARCASS!
SO WE *BOTH* HAVE SOMETHING TO DIE FOR! BEST YOU FINISH ME, THEN, WOLFRIDER!

FINISH ME NOW..!!
UNGH!
OOF!!
...OR I'LL MAKE YOU WISH YOU HAD!!

YOU'VE NEVER LET ME LOVE YOU AS I'D LIKE.
I SWORE TO DEFEND YOU... *FROM* YOU... IF NEED BE.

TIME TO REST... TIME TO DREAM A DIFFERENT DREAM...

...BELOVED!
CURSE YOU! CURSE YOUR HOLLOW BONES...

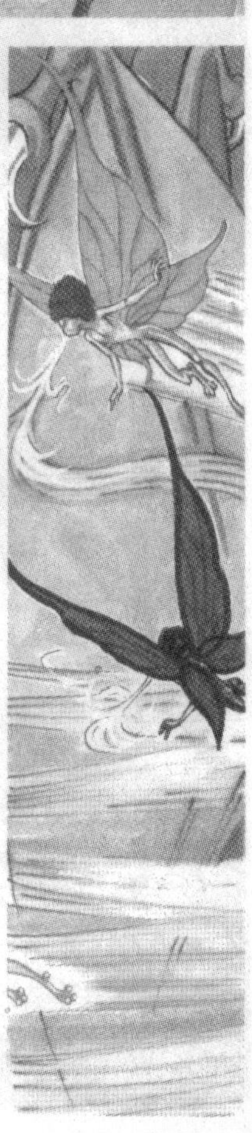

SAVAH... THIS IS YUN. SHE COULD HAVE FLED, BUT SHE BROUGHT THE LITTLE PALACE BACK TO US!
AS WINDKIN FAVORS HIS MOTHER IN SIZE AND SPIRIT...
SO, I THINK, YOU FAVOR YOUR FATHER, YUN.
H-HOW LONG... WILL KAHVI AND TYLDAK..?
WHO KNOWS? BUT WHAT BETTER WAY FOR THEM TO COOL OFF?
IF IT'S ALL RIGHT... I THINK I'LL WAIT HERE FOR THEM. I'VE NEVER SEEN THE DESERT BEFORE, OR SUCH STRANGE LODGES...
...OR EVEN STARS AS BRIGHT AS YOURS...

"A DIFFERENT SUNRISE"

"SEA-QUEEN A'BORNING"
WENDY ©90 PINI

"STRANGE ALLIES"

"TURNS BEYOND COUNTING"

"CONFRONTATION"

"THE BROKEN WHEEL"

IN THE
NEXT VOLUME

The Grand Quest comes to a whirlwind conclusion with a selection of stories featuring tales of the Wolfriders as they try to cope in their new world, and a climactic knock-down, drag-out fight between Cutter and Rayek that has been brewing for centuries!

Look for this latest addition to the DC Comics library of ElfQuest stories in

APRIL 2006

THE ELFQUEST LIBRARY FROM DC COMICS

COMPACT EDITIONS

WOLFRIDER:
Volumes One-Two

THE GRAND QUEST:
Volumes One-Thirteen

THE GRAND QUEST:
Volume Fourteen
(coming in April)

VOLUME SIX
6 ELFQUEST: THE GRAND QUEST
WENDY & RICHARD PINI

ARCHIVE EDITIONS

VOLUME ONE
VOLUME TWO
VOLUME THREE

GRAPHIC NOVELS

SEARCH THE GRAPHIC NOVELS SECTION OF DCCOMICS.COM FOR ART AND INFO ON EVERY ONE OF OUR HUNDREDS OF BOOKS! CALL 1-888-COMIC BOOK FOR THE NEAREST COMICS SHOP OR GO TO YOUR LOCAL BOOK STORE.